Criminal Justice
Recent Scholarship

Edited by
Marilyn McShane and Frank P. Williams III

A Series from LFB Scholarly

Wrongful Capital Convictions and the Legitimacy of the Death Penalty

Karen S. Miller

LFB Scholarly Publishing LLC
New York 2006

Library of Congress Cataloging-in-Publication Data

Miller, Karen S., 1968-
  Wrongful capital convictions and the legitimacy of the death penalty /
Karen S. Miller.
    p. cm. -- (Criminal justice (LFB Scholarly Publishing LLC))
  Includes bibliographical references and index.
  ISBN 1-59332-140-6 (alk. paper)
  1. Capital punishment--United States. I. Title. I. Series.
  HV8699.U6M55 2006
  364.660973--dc22

2005036161

ISBN 1-59332-140-6

Printed on acid-free 250-year-life paper.

Manufactured in the United States of America.

Contents

Acknowledgments

There are countless people whose efforts facilitated the completion of this project. For their kind efforts, I thank the staffs of: the Columbus, Mississippi Public Library; the Kansas City Public Library; the Wheeler Basin Regional Library in Decatur, Alabama; the Alabama Department of Archives and History; and the Alachua County Library District in Gainesville, Florida. My deepest appreciation goes to the Interlibrary Loan department and the Justice and Safety Library at Eastern Kentucky University. Quite simply, this project could not have been completed without their efforts. I also thank the Justice and Safety Research Center at Eastern Kentucky University for funding this project. Finally, I would like to thank Vic Kappeler, Scott Hunt, and Bill Skinner for their thoughtful feedback and guidance.

CHAPTER 1

The Legitimation Crisis

The death penalty is a public policy issue that has generated extensive scholarly research, public debate, and legal attention. It is an issue that can provoke intense emotions and heated exchanges. While individuals on both sides of the issue often have strong feelings about it, polls suggest that a majority of Americans support the death penalty in the abstract. This support fluctuates, but overall, the public has historically tended to support the notion of capital punishment (Bohm, 2003). This is not surprising. Support for punishment in general and the death penalty in particular are part of the hegemonic ideology of the United States. The state presents crime and punishment in a way that reinforces an ideology supportive of the death penalty. Maintaining and reinforcing the dominant ideology begins with the legitimation of the state's ability to punish.

LEGITIMIZING PUNISHMENT

The state legitimates its "punishment" function in three primary ways. First, it focuses attention on the crimes of the poor (Reiman, 1998). In doing so, it presents an inaccurate "reality" of crime. Since the 1960s the United States has declared wars on drugs and "crime." The war on drugs has consistently been directed at residents of inner cities and impoverished rural areas. These powerless groups form a majority of prison inmates, and the war on drugs has led to the highest incarceration rates in the world (Kappeler, Blumberg and Potter, 2000). The war on crime was directed at street criminality and led to Draconian mandatory sentencing for non-violent offenders (Beckett and Sasson, 2000). It has removed discretion from judges and reinforced the notion that America's crime problem rests with the poor.

Despite the fact that white collar crime is more damaging to society in terms of financial costs, personal injuries and even deaths, there has never been a war on white collar crime (Potter and Miller-Potter, 2002). There has never been a call for 100,000 more police officers to combat price-fixing, consumer injury and death due to negligence in manufacturing, or to combat corporate executives who steal from employee pensions. The state focuses its attention and resources on crimes of the poor. The most significant result of this focus is that it deflects attention from social inequalities and macro explanations for street-level criminality (Reiman, 1998).

The state further legitimizes its punishment function by presenting street crime as a public problem that threatens the moral order. Presenting crime as an omnipresent threat leads to a reality of fear (Altheide, 2000). Those who are fearful of fellow citizens are more trusting of the state and its social policies. In making citizens fearful of victimization of certain types of crimes the state reinforces its role as protector of society. This legitimizes the state's ability to use force. The state effectively presents crime as a threat which encourages members of society to support its response to law violators. This legitimation technique serves the purpose of deflecting attention from social inequalities and social factors that impact criminality, but it also maintains a divide between classes.

Finally, the state legitimizes punishment through the creation and maintenance of dangerous classes (Shelden, 2001). Offenders are presented as being different from other members of society. They are presented as individuals who do not aspire to achieve the American dream. "Criminals" are social trash. They are dregs, rabble, or lowlifes who have proven that they cannot live in a civil society (Shelden, 2001; Irwin, 1985). The state has effectively created a criminal/non-criminal dichotomy. This is despite the fact that an overwhelming majority of Americans have participated in behaviors that could have resulted in imprisonment (Kappeler and Potter, 2005). Instead of criminals being viewed as those who were caught participating in deviant acts, "criminals" are bad, law-breaking, norm violating, disruptive individuals who threaten the moral order of society.

These three factors encourage and reinforce an ideology that is supportive of the state's ability to punish. They also serve as the foundation for the legitimation of specific forms of punishment, particularly the death penalty. When the public is fearful of victimization of specific types of crime by certain types of people, legitimizing the penalties for situations that meet those criteria becomes an easier task. Since the groundwork has been laid the state must only show that a particular case meets those criteria. The state's legitimation of punishment plays a key role in the legitimation of the death penalty. There are, however, other techniques specific to capital punishment. Essentially, the state must carefully balance the fact that the death penalty is the epitome of legitimate state power with the notion that it serves to protect citizens and punish criminals. This requires the delegitimation of any perceived injustices and inequalities while simultaneously legitimizing the "protective" role of the system.

The death penalty is legitimized as policy in three ways. First, the state presents the death penalty as a punitive measure imposed in only the worst cases. System functionaries and politicians rarely speak of capital punishment as a public policy. They seldom present it as having geographic, victim, and offender based patterns of implementation. Those acting on behalf of the state present the death penalty as punishment meted out to individuals who commit particularly heinous crimes, or to those who have had multiple chances to prove their ability to function in a civil society. For example, when John Edwards sought the Democratic Presidential nomination in 2004 he revealed that he supports the death penalty because some crimes are so heinous they "deserve the ultimate punishment," (Zeleny and Zuckman, 2004). This is the primary factor that legitimates the continued use of capital punishment, though others are also necessary.

Second, the state further legitimizes capital punishment by presenting it as in the best interest of society. Specifically, it presents death eligible crimes as threats to the moral order, or as public problems. This includes a dichotomous representation of defendants and victims. Defendants are considered different from others in society and victims are as undeserving of the violence they encountered. These factors function to legitimize the death penalty for a particular case and as policy. Third, it is vital to the legitimacy of capital punishment that it be viewed as fair and accurate. To this end, the state claims that the capital punishment system is replete with procedural justice, due process, and equality under the law. While citizens are concerned with fairness, it is most important that the correct person be punished.

Legitimacy, therefore, also requires that measures be in place to protect against a wrongful execution. The presence of appeals and other review courts demonstrates that the state takes extreme precautions to construct a fair, just system. Appellate courts serve as the veneer of procedural justice. Their presence is necessary to maintain the notion that the system of justice is fair and equitable. It is when these safety mechanisms work to reveal errors, or to recognize those found by others, that it presents a potential legitimacy crisis for the state.

THE CRISIS

A legitimation crisis emerged from a series of highly publicized releases from death row in the late 1990s. These releases spawned a new dynamic in the debate over the use of capital punishment in the United States. Anti-death penalty organizations worked to publicize the issue and even held a conference on wrongful convictions in Chicago. The location was not randomly chosen, it was based on the fact that nine exonerations had occurred in Illinois by 1996. The organizers of the conference brought together many of the exonerated from across the country for the first time. Their photographs and stories were published in newspapers all over the world and the innocence issue suddenly became a part of the public consciousness (Bendavid, 1998).

Shortly after the conference and more importantly, after Illinois' eleventh exoneration, former Governor George Ryan called for a moratorium on executions in that state. He formed a research commission that was charged with examining the death penalty process in Illinois. The Governor's Commission on Capital Punishment (2002) concluded that it would be impossible to have a system free of errors. The Commission's report and the fact that the state legislature did not enact any of the commission's proposed reforms, led Governor Ryan to review the cases of all 167 Illinois death row inmates. During the final days of his term, Governor Ryan pardoned four inmates whom he believed were wrongfully convicted and commuted the death sentences of 163 others (Slater, 2003).

Capital exonerations are a serious challenge to the legitimacy of both death sentencing and the criminal justice system. Public opinion polls indicate that 95 percent of Americans believe that innocent people are sometimes convicted of murder (Harris Interactive Survey, 2004). Eighty percent believe an innocent person has been executed in the

United States since 1995, and 46 percent believe an innocent person was executed in Texas while George W. Bush was Governor (CNN/USA Today/Gallup Poll, 2000). This recognition of mistakes in cases with the highest legal standards has impacted public support for executions.

While support for capital punishment fluctuates, the level of support among the public has consistently declined over the last ten years (Bohm, 2003). Public opinion polls reveal that recent reductions in support levels are tied to questions of fairness in the process and wrongful convictions (Unnever and Cullen, 2005). For example, a recent Harris poll (2004) indicates that wrongful homicide convictions directly reduce respondents' support for capital punishment. An NBC News/Wall Street Journal Poll (2000) revealed that 63 percent of respondents favored a moratorium on executions in light of death row exonerations. These polls are indicative of the legitimacy crisis confronting the American system of capital punishment.

Importantly, researchers have documented the role of innocence cases in diminished public support for capital punishment. Unnever and Cullen (2005) revealed a direct link between reduced public support for capital punishment among those who believe an innocent person has been executed in recent years. Similarly, Fan, Keltner, and Wyatt (2002, p. 429) found that the "change in death penalty support" from the 1970s until the early 1990s "was in fact due to the press turning a spotlight on the condemnation of innocent persons." Reduced support for capital punishment has impacted the number of death sentences returned by juries. The number of new death sentences in the United States reached a 30 year low in 2003 (BJS, 2004). The number of men and women sent to death row in 2003 was 24 fewer than in 2002. It was less than half the annual average of new death sentences handed down in the years between 1994 and 2000.

Quite simply, the American system of capital punishment is facing a legitimacy crisis in the wake of high profile capital exonerations. While researchers have begun to examine the issue of wrongful convictions, the situation has yet to be examined as a catalyst for a legitimacy crisis. While several studies have examined the role various 'system' factors play in trial court error, wrongful convictions, death sentences, and exonerations (see Huff, 2004; Warden 2002; 2003; Miller-Potter, 2002; Harmon, 2001; Liebman, Fagan and West, 2000;

Dieter, 1997; Radelet and Bedau, 1987; Radin, 1964; Gardner, 1952, Frank and Frank, 1957; Borchard, 1932) no one has examined the state's management of this crisis. Further, numerous researchers have examined the media's role in constructing society's "reality" of crime, criminals and justice issues (see for example: Potter and Kappeler, 1996; Warr, 1995; Barak, 1994; Ericson, Baranek and Chan, 1989; Graber, 1980). The research surrounding the social construction of capital punishment issues, however, has focused on very specific aspects of homicide and/or executions. No study has attempted to combine the issues of innocence and the media and no study has attempted a longitudinal review of the media's representation of capital cases. This examination of 1044 newspaper accounts of 29 capital crimes that occurred during or after 1985 and resulted in exonerations prior to December 31, 2002 fills those gaps. It does so by using Habermas' theory of legitimation crisis to explore two basic questions.

First, I sought to determine if the local newspaper accounts of these cases presented information in ways that supported capital punishment for particular defendants in particular cases. If the articles legitimized the death penalty in a particular case, they legitimized the death penalty in the abstract. Quite simply, as long as one person deserves the death penalty, or one crime calls for it, the death penalty is legitimized as public policy. Second, if legitimating factors were present, how were they reconstructed as the story changed? The central hypothesis is that the articles functioned to legitimize the death penalty during every phase, but that the changes in legitimation techniques would coincide with the exonerations. An underlying assumption that guided these questions was that the media was the avenue through which the state would send its messages.

HABERMAS' THEORY

Habermas (1975) identified four types of crisis tendencies in late capitalism. He categorized them as economic, rationality, legitimation, and motivation. Each crisis tendency is located within three basic subsystems. These subsystems include the economic, administrative, and the socio-cultural. The crisis of capital exonerations falls within the socio-cultural. Habermas (1975, p. 48) defined the socio-cultural subsystem as including "legal and administrative acts, public and social security, etc." A crisis in the socio-cultural subsystem is prompted by changes that cannot be reconciled "by the existing supply of legitimation" (Habermas, 1975, p. 48). More specifically, a legitimation crisis within the socio-cultural subsystem is generated by society's recognition of a system's limitations or when a system's activity becomes politicized (1975, p. 50). By Habermas' definition, the exonerations of 112 death row inmates in a 27 year period has the potential to create a legitimation crisis. It is, however, society's reaction to the exonerations that produced a true crisis. Reduced public support for capital punishment and the fewer death sentences meted out by juries are the manifestations of the crisis. The crisis generated by wrongful convictions threatens the state's ability to use force against its citizens.

Weber (1958, p. 78) argued that the state is defined through "its monopoly of the legitimate use of force" and that "force is a means specific to the state." This characteristic is true of all states, though it is of special significance to the United States. The United States is the last remaining industrialized western nation to use the death penalty against its citizens for the crime of murder (Bohm, 2003). Other nations have completely abolished the death penalty through law, or ended it in practice. Additionally, abolitionist nations have also recently implemented formal policies designed to refuse extradition of defendants to the United States when the death penalty is a sentencing option. Despite the fact that the United States is under some external pressure to abolish the death penalty, its implementation continues unabated.

Historically, the United States has been able to avoid legitimation crises in the system of capital punishment by responding to concerns before a true crisis situation developed. The retention of capital punishment in the United States has not been without difficulty. From time to time Americans have expressed concerns over an issue involved in capital sentencing and executions, but the system has responded in ways that avoided true crises. In the early 1970s, following the civil rights movement, racism in sentencing was of great concern. This concern culminated in the Supreme Court's *Furman v. Georgia* (1972) ruling, which found that then existing statutes were unconstitutional due to their arbitrary and capricious application and their great potential for racial discrimination. Since the Court reinstated capital punishment in 1976 (*Gregg v. Georgia*) new issues emerged that have caused courts and legislatures to continue the reconstruction and reformulation of death penalty law. When members of society began to view electrocution as cruel and unusual punishment, states began using lethal injections (Bedau, 1997). When public opinion polls revealed that a majority of Americans opposed executing the mentally retarded, the Supreme Court banned this practice (*Atkins v. Virginia*, 2002). Even more recently, when polls indicated that the public opposed the execution of juvenile offenders, the Supreme Court deemed the practice unconstitutional (*Roper v. Simmons*, 2005). The Court's 2005 ruling came despite a history of allowing juvenile executions (see *Stanford v. Kentucky*, 1989; *Thompson v. Oklahoma*, 1988). In short, the courts and legislators respond to public outcries of cruel and unusual punishment. In listening and responding to these concerns they are legitimizing capital punishment and preventing crises that could lead to abolition. The United States is, however, now facing an unprecedented potential crisis within its socio-cultural subsystem due to its death penalty policies. Essentially, the process of legitimizing capital punishment is an ongoing one and makes Habermas' (1975) theory of legitimation crisis a useful avenue for exploring media accounts of capital cases in a capitalist society.

In capitalist societies the economic system is the principal steering mechanism. An individual's relationship to the means of production determines their class situation (Marx, 2000a). The economic system steers social formations through resources and power, but also through ideology. The hegemonic ideology of a capitalist society serves the interest of the ruling elite (Marx and Engels, 2000). The preservation of hegemony requires the legitimation of state power. Legitimation secures conformity among the ruled. Without widespread conformity the state's power and ability to control is greatly reduced. Habermas (1975) describes legitimation as the ways a government or social system justifies its existence and power. All states must legitimize their power. In modern industrial capitalist societies legitimation is primarily achieved through the idea that the government represents the will of the people. This notion is achieved through democratic elections, constitutions, representative governments, and legal statutes.

The three sub-systems identified by Habermas (1975) interact to maintain conformity among the majority. These systems, the economic, political, and socio-cultural, must be closely related and in balance to achieve legitimacy. The economic system involves subjugating conflicts between market forces and assuaging the inequalities created by exploitation of labor and class divisions. The political system involves the maintenance of popular support and loyalty. The socio-cultural system must maintain an ideological climate that supports capitalism. If any of these sub-systems fails to meet its goals a crisis will occur.

In the tradition of Marx (2000a, 2000b), Habermas (1975) argues that the capitalist system is replete with inherent contradictions due to its very design. It is organized to foster inequality rather than to provide equal access to wealth for all participants. It is driven by exploitation rather than equality. These contradictions lead to a permanent state of crisis management that is balanced by one sub-system compensating for the weaknesses of another. When the weaknesses of a sub-system become unmanageable, a crisis occurs. A crisis is a point at which the legitimacy of a social, political or economic system is strained and, therefore, questioned (Habermas, 1975). The avoidance of crisis is imperative. The state must maintain support among the masses. The majority must view the state and its policies as legitimate. The establishment and maintenance of legitimacy is achieved through ideological control. The state and cultural apparatuses must convince the majority that the existing system is rational, equitable, and legitimate (Habermas, 1975).

More specifically, and in the tradition of Weber (1968), Habermas (1975, p. 95-102) addresses the legitimacy of authority as it applies to law. Weber argued that legitimacy of authority requires the establishment of normative order, and that members of society must view the process of law creation as legitimate. Societal acceptance of law creation is described as "legal positivism" and requires "a general consensus grounded in a rational orientation to value" (Habermas, 1975, p. 99). "Legal positivism" can only achieve legitimacy when it can be shown to include "formal procedures" that "fulfill material claims to justice under certain institutional boundary conditions" (Habermas, 1975, p. 99). Essentially, the legitimacy of law and punishment require procedural due process. As the ultimate punishment, the death penalty, requires heightened legal review to be accepted as legitimate.

The theory of crisis legitimation provides a foundation for analyzing how legitimation occurs in a class-based society. Habermas (1975) argues that legitimation in a system of opposing classes is primarily based on the belief that similar opportunities exist for all members and that only those who conform will succeed. This notion is the foundation of the ideological hegemony of the United States' ruling elite. Americans are socialized from a young age to believe that hard work and conformity will lead to a successful, financially rewarding life. The "American Dream" encourages members of society to ignore the injustices experienced by others. It offers an individual explanation for a multitude of injustices. This legitimizes both the state and social inequalities, and redirects attention from macro social forces and removes responsibility from both the state and society.

The criminal justice system is but one of a multitude of institutions that legitimizes the state in this way. As a system of punishment it is designed to control those who do not conform. As a system of policies, it is designed to appeal to those who do. The criminal justice system acts to divide members of the same class situation and to further divide members of different classes. This is accomplished through the establishment and maintenance of fear among one class of another (Shelden, 2001; Altheide, 2002). The criminal justice system serves the interest of state legitimacy, but it is also a tool used to maintain ideological hegemony.

CHAPTER 2

Constructing Legitimacy

Producing and maintaining an ideology that recognizes the legitimacy of punishment first involves creating a social reality of crime. Quinney (1970) argues that a social reality is created, experienced, and believed in by a group. A social reality is the aggregate of knowledge, experience, and ideas (Quinney, 1970). It is generally agreed that there are four sources of the knowledge on which social reality is constructed: personal experience, significant others, social groups and institutions, and mass media (Surette, 1998, p. 6). Experienced reality consists of all the events directly encountered. The other three sources form a symbolic reality. Symbolic knowledge facilitates the formation of abstract ideas. It is the symbolic transfer of cultural knowledge. From this combination of sources social reality is constructed. The degree to which the media shapes reality is directly impacted by the availability of the other sources (Surette, 1998). The fact that most people do not experience most events firsthand, however, creates an increased reliance on the media to shape "reality." While the media is vital to constructions of reality, it is overly simplistic to argue that the media is solely responsible.

In the construction of a general social reality, the media is one part of a complex matrix that influences the conceptions of reality. It is likely that interaction with peers and family have a greater impact than the media on perceptions of general social phenomenon. For specific issues, however, the role of the media increases. This is especially true of crime and justice issues because most people never experience violent crime firsthand (Altheide, 2002; Barkan, 2001; Kappeler, et al., 2000; Potter and Kappeler, 1996). It is also likely that most people never experience violent crime through those they know. The media's presentation of crime, however, has constructed a social reality of crime that is distorted on many levels.

The "reality" constructed by the media often directly contradicts the reality of crime (Altheide, 2002; Barkan, 2001; Kappeler, et al., 2000; Potter and Kappeler, 1996). This is primarily achieved through the amplification of certain types of crimes (Surette, 1998; Potter and Kappeler, 1996). For example, stranger child abductions, murders by serial killers, and stranger rapes are more heavily reported than similar crimes perpetrated by those known to the victims (Kappeler and Potter, 2005; Kappeler, et al., 2000; Jenkins, 2000; Best, 1999). The amplification of these relatively rare crimes impacts the "reality" of crime that is constructed (Kappeler, et al., 2000; Surette, 1998; Potter and Kappeler, 1996). The focus on these "sensational" crimes also functions to reinforce crime's threat to the moral order and the maintenance of dangerous classes (Altheide, 2002; Shelden, 2001; Kappeler, et al., 2000).

Research clearly indicates that the public's knowledge and information about crime, criminals, victims, crime policies, and the criminal justice system come from the mass media (Graber, 1980; Ericson, Baranek and Chan, 1989; Barak, 1994; Warr, 1995; Potter and Kappeler, 1996). The media's focus on crime and the fact that most people get their information about crime from the media are the factors that converge to impact society's "reality" of crime. Studies show that 20% of local television news programming, 13% of national news programming, and 25% of newspaper space is devoted to crime and law enforcement (Ericson et al. 1989; Surette 1998; Potter and Kappeler 1996). Media outlets tend to make violent crime the foundation of their crime news. For example, Sheley and Ashkins (1981) found that only 20% of index crime reported in New Orleans involved violence while 68% of newspaper crime stories focused on violent crimes. Similar results have been found in Chicago (Graber 1980) and nationally (Liska and Baccaglini 1990).

SELECTING "NEWS"

The fact that the media over reports violent crime does not mean that all violent crimes are reported. It also does not mean that what is reported receives the same amount of space and page placement. News selection is impacted by numerous internal organizational and external forces. Internal factors such as deadlines, staffing, and investigative resources all impact the content of news (Surette, 1998). Selection of news largely depends on how the event connects with prior news, themes, and accepted public explanations (Surette, 1998). The fact that "news" is "selected" means that to some degree, "news" is subjective. Not all events that could be presented as news are reported. Hall (1984; Hall, Critcher, Jefferson, Clarke and Roberts, 1978) noted that news reporters speak of "news" as if the important news, angles and events are self-selecting. In reality, an individual reporter and/or editor determines if something will be reported, and how much attention it will receive. The choice of events reported, those chosen as important, and the angles used are filtered through the ideological atmosphere of society.

Marx and Engels (2000) argued that the hegemonic ideology of any era is the ideology of the dominant class. Quinney (1979, p. 35) posited that the dominant group in a capitalist society "expands its influence by perpetuating a particular conception of reality." Schudson (1991) argued that the ideological atmosphere of a society is created by dominant groups and institutions and that the presentation of news is supportive of their ideology. Gans (1979) argues that for American journalism the values associated with the hegemonic ideology include ethnocentrism, altruism, responsible capitalism, individualism, and moderatism. While each of these orientations plays an important role in news selection and production, moderatism is especially significant (Hertog and McLeod, 2001). Hall (1984) posits that in a capitalist society there are two extreme views. At one end of the spectrum is extremely conservative support for the dominant ideology. At the other end is the extremely liberal, anti-establishment view. Hall (1984) argues that the media is biased towards the dominant or consensual values of society with a right-leaning bent. Essentially, he posits that the ideas promoted by the media fall somewhere between the status quo and the political right, and the ideas that subvert the existing power structure tend to be ignored or treated as nuisances (Hall, 1984). While ideological considerations are an important factor in news selection, others are also important.

According to Altheide (2002) frames and formats also shape the content of mass media. Where formats relate to time, space and manner, frames are broad thematic emphases (Altheide, 1976). A central part of the shaping of news is the development of formats, or the way it is selected, organized and presented (Altheide, 2002). The formats become recognizable to and even expected by audiences. Altheide (2002) also argues that packaged news forms insinuate newsworthiness, which facilitates audience acceptance of an item as news. Framing, in this context, refers to the parameters for discussing a particular news item. It is important that an item fit into the format chosen by a media outlet. Hertog and McLeod (2001, 141) describe frames as "cultural rather than cognitive phenomena." They argue that as cultural structures, frames have symbolic power, excess meaning, and widespread recognition. Most importantly, frames determine the relevant content of a social problem, structure society's understanding of a phenomenon, and describe the relationship between issues, among others.

The factors that impact the selection of news also impact the amount of attention paid to a particular story. Newspaper reports of crime fall into four categories: tertiary, secondary, primary and super primary (Chermak, 1995a). Tertiary stories are typically space fillers, less than 5 inches in space, and rarely contain by-lines. These stories tend to be in columns titled "regional," "state," or "local" briefs. Secondary stories are somewhat fuller accounts that include a reporter by-line. They are often on the inner or back pages and given 6-12 inches in print space. Primary stories are rather high profile stories that are on the front page or the front page of the local section. They are more in-depth accounts and often target a larger community concern. Super primary stories are those that are newsworthy at a national or even international level. Stories of this nature often include related items on the same or following pages (Chermak, 1995a, 32-40). In sum, the nature of what is reported, as well as how it is reported, are affected by the daily functioning of media outlets, other news events, and ideology. News selection is also impacted by the sensational nature of the event.

Research of the media's presentation of crime indicates that it tends to focus on sensational crimes, which often means homicide (Chermak, 1995a; Chermak, 1995b; Potter and Kappeler, 1996; Sheley and Ashkins, 1981). Again, this focus reinforces the notion that crime is a threat to the moral order. These studies indicate that news coverage overrepresents the occurrence of homicide and that this overrepresentation impacts prosecutorial decisions regarding charges filed and plea bargains offered (Pritchard, 1986; Kappeler, et al., 2000; Potter and Kappeler, 1996). For example, Pritchard (1986) reviewed 90 homicide cases in Milwaukee County, Wisconsin for an 18-month period in the early 1980s. The review focused on the level of newspaper interest in the case and whether or not it impacted the prosecutors decision to plea bargain. Pritchard (1986) concluded that the average length of stories was the strongest predictor of plea bargains, with more extensive coverage making it less likely that the prosecutor would negotiate with the defendant.

Sheley and Ashkins (1981) found that while homicide accounted for only 0.4% of felonies known to the New Orleans police, it accounted for 12% of newspaper crime stories and 50% of television crime stories. A study in Chicago found that murder represented only 0.2% of crimes reported to the police, but constituted 26.2% of all news stories about crime (Graber 1980). At the national level, Liska and Baccaglini (1990) found that in twenty-six cities, homicides accounted for .02% of crimes known to the police, but were featured in 30% of all crime stories. While the media overreports homicide, it also focuses on the most sensational murders, particularly those involving multiple victims (Jenkins, 2000; Potter and Kappeler 1996; Box 1983). For example, Chermak (1998a) examined 1557 crime stories from the six large and mid-size regional newspapers. Using multiple regression techniques, he found that the number of victims affected by a crime was the best predictor of increased story salience, i.e. how long the story is covered. Other researchers revealed similar results.

In a review of homicide reports in two Chicago daily papers, Johnstone, Hawkins, and Michener (1994) found that the papers focused on "high-amplitude homicides," or those involving multiple victims, males charged with killing females, white victims, and/or occurred in affluent neighborhoods. Paulsen (2003) compared homicide data in Houston, Texas to reports in appearing in the *Houston Chronicle*. He found that the paper focused on cases involving statistically rare scenarios of female victims, female offenders, multiple victims and multiple offenders. Other studies have found similar results (Wilbanks, 1984; Pritchard and Hughes, 1997; Sorenson, Manz, and Berk, 1998; Weiss and Chermak, 1998).

Duwe (2000) also examined media accounts of mass homicides. He focused on mass murders between 1976 and 1996 in his review of accounts found in newspapers, network television news, and newsweekly magazines. He found that these stories tended to be newsworthy on a local level but only received national attention when they involved large numbers of victims, stranger victims, public locations, assault weapons, workplace violence, and interracial victim-offender characteristics. Duwe (2000) concluded that the situations that received high-profile attention were the most extreme and atypical of the cases. He argued that the media focuses on these cases in an effort to maximize their audience and profits by catering to society's fascination with sensational acts of violence. The research in this regard supports the idea that the media's focus on these "high amplitude" homicides reinforces an ideology supportive of punishment. It facilitates the criminal/non-criminal dichotomy, and reinforces the notion that some crimes meet the heinousness standard for the ultimate punishment.

Reports of crime and the space devoted to crime by the media are also impacted by victim and offender characteristics (Lundman, 2003; Paulsen, 2003; Chermak, 1995a; Chermak, 1995b). With regard to typical reports of crime, the media often ignores victims of crime unless they are particularly sympathetic, have a distinguishing characteristic, or are willing to cooperate with storytelling efforts. In his examination of the role victims play in the production of crime news, Chermak (1995a) found that victim and defendant demographics are rarely reported in crime news. He established that victim race was revealed in 15% of stories while defendant race was revealed in 25%. The age of the victim was almost always revealed, while marital status and occupation were rarely reported. He argued that the primary reason for this related to ease of access to the information. Essentially, reporters could easily determine the victim's age from police reports while occupation and other demographic information was more difficult to obtain. Chermak (1995a) found victim occupation was reported in 30% of crime stories, but that it was most likely to be reported if it involved a criminal justice system worker, a politician, or student. Chermak's research also revealed that the victimization of married people was more likely to be reported than if the victim was single or divorced. He determined that victimizations of females, whites, and the young were overreported, and that crime in suburban areas was more newsworthy than inner-city crime.

While reports of victimizations of females are overrreported, the type of information included in reports appears to be impacted by victim gender. Anastasio and Costa (2004) reviewed 148 newspaper reports of violent crimes and concluded that victims were presented differently based on their gender. They revealed that violent crime reports tended to provide more personal information about male than female victims. Anastasio and Costa (2004) determined that male victims were more likely to be referred to by name, while female victims were more likely to be referred to as "the victim."

Victim race also impacts newsworthiness. Chermak (1998b) reviewed 227 *Indianapolis Star* reports of homicides between 1995 and 1996. He found that homicides involving white victims averaged 2.7 articles while cases involving African-American victims averaged 2.06 articles. He also determined that more words were written about murders with multiple victims, white victims, and female victims. In short, he found that homicides involving white victims were given preferential treatment by the local print media. Chermak (1998b) concluded that providing more coverage of homicides involving white victims perpetuates the devaluation of African-American victimization.

Others have also noted that minority victimization is underrepresented. For example, Paulsen (2003) found that incidents involving African-American or Hispanic victims were significantly less likely to be reported than white victims. In a review of hate crimes reports in two Chicago daily papers Protess (1993) found that reports focused on incidents involving African-American offenders and white victims. This focus was despite the fact that the majority of hate crimes during the study period involved white perpetrators and African-American victims. Similarly, Lundman (2003) argues that race, gender and their intersection are important components of journalistic notions of newsworthiness.

Victim and defendant demographics clearly impact media outlets' conceptions of newsworthiness of crime stories. Ultimately, however, victim cooperation and quality can provide the element that makes a crime newsworthy. If these things are absent a story may not be reported. The significance of the effects of the victims and defendants chosen for news reports is not only the devaluation of minority victimization. Overreporting certain types of crimes against certain types of people are instrumental in constructing and maintaining a social reality of fear.

CONSTRUCTING FEAR

The results of Chermak's (1998a; 1998b) Paulsen's (2003) and Protess (1993) research also support the idea that the media presents crime as threatening the moral order. Altheide (2002) argues that the media's focus on crimes of violence has led to a social reality of fear. While it is difficult to determine if public fear precedes crime reporting or vice versa, a Finnish study (Kivivuori, Kemppi, and Smolej, 2002) supports Altheide's (2002) hypothesis. The authors compared tabloid newspaper reports of crime between 1988 and 1997 to fear of crime surveys for the same period. They found that crime and victimization rates declined during this period, but reports of crime increased in their intensity of reporting, use of photographs, prominence of headlines and front page placement. The level of crime fear increased with the prominence of crime reports. (Kivivuoir et al., 2002).

In a random survey of California residents, Lane and Meeker (2003) established that primary sources of crime information impact levels of fear. They found that newspapers were the primary source of crime news for white respondents and that newspaper content had a negative effect on their levels of fear of crime and perceived risk. They established that television had the same effect on Hispanics who reported television as their primary news source. Similarly, Heath (1984) found that newspaper stories that focus on random violent crimes led to an increase of public fear of crime. A study with similar results was conducted in Phoenix (Baker, Nienstedt, Everett, and McCleary, 1983).

The distorted reality of crime has impacted the level of fear of crime among Americans (Altheide, 2002). This preoccupation with fear serves a very important purpose, it prevents people from questioning the nature of social order. It does this by directing the public's attention to specific crimes, which facilitates the establishment of those crimes as true social problems. The net effect of a social reality of fear is that it legitimates punishment. A fearful public is more accepting of formal social control initiatives and more readily believes that those who violate societal norms are different. This notion is also supported by research on the media's presentation of criminal defendants.

As previously discussed, the defendant characteristics can greatly impact the newsworthiness of a crime. The defendant or suspect is often presented as the evil preying on the innocent of society (Surette, 1992). In a review of media reports of crime, Graber (1980) recognized that defendants were presented as violent predators, politicians, or bureaucrats. Chermak's (1995a) research supported this typology. He concluded that young males are most likely to be presented as predators in crime news and that when defendant occupation was reported, it was usually a politician or professional.

Others view defendant representation differently. Reiman (1998) argues that the types of crimes reported by the media provide the false impression that crime is overwhelmingly committed by young, poor, minority, mostly urban males. Others have disputed this claim. For example, Chermak (1995a) argues that a defendant attributed higher status in a community can greatly impact the newsworthiness of a crime. He also determined that white defendants were more likely than minority defendants to be presented as primary news. In any event, the defendant is central to crime news. Chermak (1995a) found that the defendant was mentioned in 92% of stories, only being absent when the crime had not been cleared by arrest or an arrest was not imminent.

Paulsen's (2003) review of newspaper accounts of homicides revealed that female offenders were slightly more represented in the paper than males. He found similar patterns based on defendant race. Specifically, he revealed that 66% of homicides involving white offenders were reported even though they accounted for only 13% of the homicides during the study period. Further, Asians represented only 2% of homicide suspects yet 78% of these incidents were reported (Paulsen, 2003). Similarly, Chermak (1998b) determined that cases involving female suspects averaged one additional article per case and that more words were written about these cases.

The research on homicide reports indicates overwhelmingly that local print media focuses on certain types of victims, offenders, and crime circumstances, all of which are statistically rare. The news media's focus on statistically rare victims, defendants, and crimes functions to produce distorted social realities of crime. These distortions reinforce the media's presentation of crime as random and senseless, which in turn impacts the level of fear. Similarly, researchers have determined the willingness of certain types of sources to participate in news production impacts the social reality of crime and the legitimacy of the system.

CLAIMSMAKERS

In its depictions of crime, the news media makes explicit and implicit claims about crime, criminals, and victims. Such activity is the focus of the claimsmaking perspective of social problems (Best, 1999; 1995; 1991; 1990). Claimsmaking theory focuses on the defining of social problems by individuals, groups, and institutions such as the news media, movie industry, social movements, government agencies and others. In modern society, the mass media is the principal avenue for making claims relating to social problems. In contemporary society, the media is the most cost effective method for reaching the largest audience. A large audience is important because claimsmaking involves both the labeling of certain issues as social problems and the identification of characteristics of the problem (Surette, 1998). Claimsmakers seek a large audience when drawing attention to an issue because it maximizes the potential to provoke social change. The potential for social change encourages claimsmakers to be the driving force in the way a problem is framed. The framing of a potential problem can originate with the media or another source.

The media is both a primary and secondary claimsmaker (Best, 1991). It is a primary claimsmaker in two ways. First, the media discovers and constructs social problems on its own. For example, Best (1991) explored the press as primary claimsmakers of freeway violence as a social problem. He reviewed the process that brought the 1987 Los Angeles freeway shootings to national prominence. He described this form of claimsmaking as involving the discovery of the problem. He argued that when a pattern was revealed, the issue became appealing because it contained drama and immediacy. The fact that the discovery was made by a prestigious newspaper during a slow news season was largely the deciding factor in the national prominence of the issue. Essentially, a regional paper manufactured a public problem that was picked up by the national media. The national media attempted to document the spread of this problem to other areas. When it was unsuccessful the problem disappeared (Best, 1991). Second, the media is also a primary claimsmaker through its choice of and presentation of crime news (Potter and Kappeler, 1996). Essentially, the media's focus on crimes of violence sends the message that crime is a threat to the moral order.

When a group or individual with an agenda takes an issue to the media for dissemination, the media acts as a secondary claimsmaker. As such, it redefines the problem according to its organizational needs. As secondary claimsmakers, the media use four primary techniques (Best, 1995). First, it uses sensationalism. This can involve a focus on relatively rare events that are presented as epidemic or at least more common than in reality. Second, the media uses stories designed to shock the public. These stories elicit an emotional response and utilize individual stories as examples of the behavior. Third, the media tends to rely on official sources. This offers credibility to the issue and to the story. Finally, the media uses typification. This is the presentation of information in a way that exaggerates the frequency of an event and/or meets its organizational goals, which primarily revolve around maximizing readers or viewers.

While the four techniques used by the media as primary claimsmakers are all important, the reliance on official sources is of special significance. Researchers have consistently documented the media's dependence on state sources (Sigal, 1973; Ericson, Baranek, and Chan, 1989; Chermak, 1995a; Chermak, 1995b; Surette, 1998; Haney and Greene, 2004). Importantly, this dependence on official sources impacts the content of news. For example, the media depends largely on the police to provide information about crimes that have been reported by citizens. The end result of this relationship is news stories that focus on police theories of crimes and their suspects (Chermak, 1995b). This does not mean that it is a conspiracy among police and reporters to present crime in a certain way, just that a symbiotic relationship exists. A reporter needs information and the police have that information. The path of least resistance requires the reporter to take that information and present it to the audience. This is much easier than tracking down and interviewing the victims, suspects, and witnesses. While the messages sent by a reliance on official sources may not be contemplated, it does enable the transmission of beliefs and values that are supportive of the hegemonic ideology (Surette, 1998). It also, however, provides an avenue for formal agents of social control to legitimize their agendas. This is particularly true of crime news (Surette, 1998).

As early as 1973, Sigal (1973) found that government officials accounted for half of the sources in the *New York Times* and *Washington Post*. The media's dependence on official sources has continued unabated since that time. Chermak (1995a) found that law enforcement and court officials constituted more than half of all sources in stories about crime. More recently, Haney and Greene (2004) found that in reports of capital homicide cases the articles primarily cited law enforcement and prosecutorial sources. While there is a long history between police and the media, the most significant development is that in recent years police agencies have increasingly utilized public information officers (PIOs) and have been taking their agendas to the media (Surette, 1998). What had traditionally been a reactive relationship with the media has become proactive. In actively participating with the dissemination of crime news, the police assure a steady stream of crime related stories, impart a social control ideology, and advance a formal social control agenda on the public, while simultaneously promoting a positive organizational and collective image (Surette, 1998; Chermak, 1995b).

The significance of the interdependent relationship between the media and police agencies lies in the presentation of crime. The news media are often merely editors of public relations releases. They rework information provided by official agencies and present a biased account of a situation (Gandy, 1980). Since the public views the police as experts on crime (Ericson, Baranek, and Chan, 1989), and a bureaucratic connection has been established, the police are readily available sources of information. Additionally, the media provides a cost-effective avenue for the dissemination of the police agenda. It allows the police and other state sources to set the tone for determining what is important about crime, the appropriate response to crime, and what crimes and offenders are newsworthy. For example, Haney and Greene (2004) concluded that the dependence on police and prosecutorial sources combined with the lack of mitigating information from defense sources undermines the social factors in crime causation and may influence public support for capital punishment. In short, the news media presents crime news that has been filtered by the police and is designed to promote traditional responses to crime (Sacco, 1995).

The research by Chermak (1995a; 1995b), Surette (1998) Ericson, Baranek and Chan (1989), Haney and Greene (2004) and Sacco (1995) clearly indicates that the media relies on state sources for its information about crime. This inter-relationship enables the state to "own" the problems of crime and justice (Gusfield, 1981). One area that has received less attention, however, is that of counterclaims. Benford and Hunt (2003) argue that public problems are framed and reframed in the public problems marketplace. They contend that attempts to frame an issue as a public problem are often met with counterframes, or "rhetorical strategies that challenge original claims or frames" (Benford and Hunt, 2003, p. 160). Counterframing occurs when original claimsmakers are faced with antagonistic forces that stand in opposition to their arguments. There are four types of counterframing processes. The first is "problem denial," or attempts by original claimers to simply deny the existence of a problem. The second technique involves "counter attributions." These are disagreements regarding the underlying causes of a problem rather than the existence of the problem. Third, "counter prognoses" recognize the existence of a problem, but offer alternative solutions. Finally, "attacks on collective character" are also reframing techniques. These involve a directed effort to discredit the antagonists' claims by attacking their collective character. The reliance on state sources and the notion of counterframing not only allows the state to reinforce its social control agenda and ideology, they also impact the media's presentation of different aspects of the criminal justice system and its functionaries.

THE SYSTEM IN THE MEDIA

Researchers have determined that various system functionaries and their roles are treated differently by the news media. Graber (1980) found that the media tends to portray the police as doing a fair job. Surette (1998) concluded that the media presents the police as heroic professional crime fighters, while simultaneously presenting them as incompetent. Others have argued that news outlets exaggerate the crime clearance rate which leads to a public perception of police as more effective than in reality (Roshier, 1973; Skogan and Maxfield, 1981; Marsh, 1991).

The correctional and court system are not treated in a similar way. Graber (1980) found that the media presents the courts and correctional system as doing poor jobs. Marsh (1991) concluded that the news media basically ignores the corrections system. News reports of corrections almost always report it in a negative way or are just reports of an execution or a riot (Turnbo, 1994; Surette, 1998). Surette (1998, p. 70) argues that news presentations of the correctional system and its components are scarce, and when they occur, they are unbalanced because they emphasize "predatory inmates and criminogenic institutions." Research on the media's presentation of prisons is relatively rare. Like media accounts, researchers have focused more on executions.

Research indicates that the media tends to focus on the sensational when reporting executions. Hochstetler (2001) reviewed the media reports of 499 executions in the United States in an effort to understand the media's influence on public opinion of capital punishment, deterrence, and the symbolic effects of this form of punishment. He concluded that the media focuses on the most sensational cases while ignoring routine executions of relatively mundane murderers. Hochstetler (2001) argues that by focusing on sensational cases, the media presents capital punishment as an efficacious crime fighting tool and adds to the level of public support for this policy.

Yanich (1997) reached a similar conclusion upon reviewing the Wilmington, Delaware and Philadelphia, Pennsylvania media coverage surrounding a 1994 Delaware execution. He argued that how the stories were presented reflected the fact that news is driven by the demands of the market. In essence, in an area where public support for the death penalty was high, the media presented the execution in a way that reinforced and agreed with public opinion. In fact, one station Yanich (1997) reviewed failed to present any debates or alternate views of capital punishment. Yanich (1997) argued that in failing to present both sides of the issue, the media perpetuates the public's support for capital punishment. The researcher of Yanich (1997) and Hochstetler (2001) research also indicates that the media's presentations of executions reinforces and legitimizes a hegemonic ideology that is supportive of punishment in general and the death penalty in particular.

CHAPTER 3

Investigating the Issues

Habermas (1975) argued that crisis is avoided by one subsystem compensating for the weaknesses of another. I have expanded his argument by attempting to show that the subsystem facing crisis can function alone to avoid true crisis. Legitimation of one subsystem does not require action of another. To this end, this study was designed to answer two primary questions. First, did the articles present information in a way that legitimized the death penalty? Second, did the legitimation techniques change as the story changed? A full understanding of these dynamics, however, required answers to two other questions. These questions revolved around informants and character representations. Specifically, how did the local print media present the crimes, victims, defendants, and system? Second, who were the dominant informants in the reports of these cases?

The collection of data involved several inter-related steps. The first issue was sampling. I sought a sample of defendants that had been convicted and processed under constitutional capital statutes.

SAMPLING

The first step in this analysis was the identification all men and women who were exonerated after receiving a death verdict after the Supreme Court's 1972 *Furman v. Georgia* ruling. Further, all cases in which the crime occurred prior to January 1, 1985 were excluded from this review. This was done for historical and practical reasons. When the United States Supreme Court declared capital punishment statutes unconstitutional in 1972 (*Furman v. Georgia*), states were compelled to rework their existing statues. In three 1976 decisions, U. S. Supreme Court reversed its position by upholding the rights of states to administer death sentencing (*Gregg v. Georgia, Jurek v. Texas*, and *Proffit v. Florida*). These 1976 decisions stipulated that states had to institute an independent procedure to adjudicate sentence after a guilty verdict is reached in capital cases. Compliance with the Supreme Court's new sentencing requirements for capital cases was not immediate. In fact, Jacobs and Carmichael (2002, p. 123) report that "four death-penalty states had not altered their statutes" by as late as 1995. The focus on cases since 1985, concentrates on cases that have emerged in a judicial climate established in the mid-1970s and early 1980s that attempted to ensure that death sentences are "warranted," and were administered under the guidelines of "constitutional" statutes.

The elimination of all cases prior to 1985 also had a practical advantage. Advances in communication technology have made newspaper stories more accessible through either direct archives or services such as Lexis-Nexis and NewsBank. These archives covered the entire case in some cases and partial dates in most. Newspaper archives and search engines made it possible to locate, access, and store electronically full text copies of the news stories relevant to this study. These advances in communication technology mean that a wider array of newspapers and their stories are more conveniently available for inquiry now than in the past. In short, these archives greatly facilitated the successful completion of this project.

The list of all capital exonerations in the post-*Furman* era was obtained from the Death Penalty Information Center (DPIC, 2002), a large, non-profit informational organization. The selection of all cases in which the initial crime was reported during or after 1985 and the exoneration occurred prior to the December 31, 2002 resulted in a population of 31. Because it was not possible to locate articles for two cases, they were treated as missing and were eliminated from the analysis. In one of the missing cases, the only library to hold microfilm would not release it through interlibrary loan. The second missing case spanned 15 years and the articles could only be retrieved by reviewing microfilm from a large regional paper. Each reel of film contained one week of newspapers. It would have required the review of 780 reels of film because I did not have significant dates in the case. Additionally, this case involved the murder of a prison inmate, therefore, it is qualitatively different from all other cases. For the remaining 29 cases, newspaper stories were gathered that pertained to the initial report of the crime, the investigation, the arrest, trial(s), and retrial(s), exoneration, and post-exoneration follow-ups (see Appendix A for individual case summaries). The identification and collection of the stories for the analysis involved several interrelated steps.

DATA GATHERING AND CODING

The first step in the data collection efforts was to gather the published opinions of the reversing courts. Only 22 opinions were collected because others were not published or the cases did not involve review court reversals. These opinions provided much useful information. Most opinions provided the date and location of the crime, the name(s) of the victim(s), and important dates in the history of the case. This information enabled a directed search of newspapers, and facilitated the second step, locating the newspaper closest to the crime. It was reasoned that the paper in closest proximity to the crime would provide the greatest coverage. Weekly papers were the exception. Four crimes occurred in locations that were covered by weekly newspapers. In three of these cases, the weekly paper was collected, as was a larger daily regional paper. This was done to assure that the complete story could be gleaned from the coverage. In one case, only the weekly paper was collected because the larger regional paper was not available.

This analysis involved articles from 29 different newspapers from 14 states representing all active death penalty regions of the country (see Appendix B for a list of newspapers). The newspapers were found by online searches of yellow pages for the relevant city or county. Three papers reported on multiple cases: the *Chicago Tribune*, the *Sun Sentinel*, and the *Tampa Tribune*. In three cases, stories from two daily papers were collected, rather than just the nearest one to the crime. This decision was made in the interest of collecting the fullest possible coverage of the incidents. In five cases, a larger regional daily paper was chosen over the local daily. This was done for ease of access to the stories and to provide a cross-section of newspaper sizes. When the closest paper was not chosen, the larger paper was identified through conversations with an employee of the smaller paper or an archivist at the local library. These individuals provided information on the newspaper with the widest readership in that county.

Third, the website for each newspaper was reviewed to determine the availability of online searchable archives or indexes and the date limits of the archives. The archives available through most newspaper websites, however, are fee based. The searches are free, but article retrieval is costly. A search was then done of Lexis-Nexis and NewsBank. These news databases were available free through the University of Kentucky library. The availability of these archives greatly reduced the financial costs associated with this project. Articles from 24 cases from 29 different newspapers were collected solely or partially through one or both of these archive services.

The fourth step involved the search for newspaper articles from online sources. The searches were tedious and time consuming. Including the review of microfilm discussed below, it took approximately two years to retrieve all the articles for this project. The searches were conducted methodically and began with a search of the victim's name the day after the crime occurred. Each online search was done using monthly parameters. For example, if the crime occurred in June, 1986 a search was done for the victim's full name for June and then July, etc. All years of each case were searched for the full name of the victim, the full name of the defendant, the last name only of each, and various phrases. These phrases were used to find articles that may not have been returned with name searches. For example, one report of a victim's death was found only by a search for "8 year-old found slain" even though the victim's name was in the article. Similar phrases were used in all cases in an attempt to locate stories potentially missed by searching for the obvious.

All cases available online included a search of the newspapers' direct archives and Lexis-Nexis and/or NewsBank. I determined that the searches of the direct archive were more consistent in their search terms. Searching the direct archive enabled the creation of a list of stories for each case. These stories were then retrieved from a free service. Searching both archives diminished the possibility of missing stories available from online search engines. All cases available through online archive searches were conducted twice. Performing two searches of both databases greatly reduced the possibility that any articles were missed.

Ten cases involved newspaper online archives that did not cover all the relevant dates and six cases were collected solely through other means. The articles available through online databases were collected using the same techniques described above. The stories that were unavailable through online sources were obtained by searching microfilm, from the newspaper's library or archive service, or local libraries. For these cases, I contacted the newspaper to determine if they maintained clippings files or indexes of stories. Larger, urban papers were most helpful in this regard. Three newspapers had clippings files of the articles or a computerized database. These articles were purchased directly from the newspaper. The costs associated with obtaining stories from the papers were exorbitant. One case required $7.50 per article, one $2.75 per copy, and another $3.50. This fee was deemed excessive because two had clippings files and just required copies be made. The most expensive were printed from the computer database that is not available to the public.

Finding stories from small, rural papers was the most difficult. None of the small papers maintained indexes or clippings files. In these cases, the local libraries were most helpful. Three local libraries maintained their own indexes and/or clippings files and the articles were purchased from the library or a local researcher was hired to retrieve them from microfilm. In one of these cases, it is possible that some articles are missing. The library had a clipping file and index, I purchased the available articles and hired a researcher to gather the indexed articles from microfilm. The articles I received, however, began with the first trial. Several requests were made through ILL to get the film from the date of the crime and arrest, but the local library would not release it and it was not held by a state library. The local researcher claimed to check the film for the days following the victim's death and the defendant's arrest but found no reports. The attention paid to the trial, retrial and exoneration indicates that the paper would have covered the victim's death. Every effort was made to get these articles, but they either did not exist or could not be found. Since this case involved the only female defendant in the population, I decided to include it in the review despite the possibility of missing articles.

One case was obtained directly from the two reporters at different newspapers who had written almost all the articles about the case. Reporter cooperation was very rare. The reporters who provided copies of the articles were the only two of 15 contacted who responded to emails or telephone calls. The most common means of obtaining the stories unavailable online, however, was to order microfilm through Interlibrary Loan (ILL). In two cases, I was able to gather a complete list of all stories from a searchable index. One list was provided from the newspaper and the other was from a local library. In these cases, obtaining the stories was relatively easy due to the known dates and page numbers. In the other cases, however, it was more difficult.

Ten cases were partially obtained from microfilm and one case was entirely collected in this way. In some cases several years of microfilm had to be searched, others involved a few weeks or months. Most state archives would only allow the release of two to six reels per request, so I requested film monthly increments of film. In an effort to speed up the process, I made requests in the names of others through two university ILL departments. This resulted in a steady stream of film and greatly reduced the time it would have taken if one person were making requests. For the case collected solely from microfilm, I reviewed all dates falling between the discovery of the crime and a year after exoneration. In all, this one case required the review of eight years of microfilm. This was possible only because the case involved a weekly paper and each reel contained six months of newspapers. In cases from large regional papers I reviewed film for all dates with the exception of the post-conviction phase.

After reviewing film for several cases, I determined that the years following conviction and prior to exonerations rarely contained stories other than reports of appeals or signing of death warrants. I obtained the dates of these events through exoneration stories that often contained "time-lines," or from court rulings. To expedite the process, I ordered film for two weeks before and after these dates. It seemed that searching around significant dates was a reasonable means of locating the stories. In these cases, I chose a two-week time period and thoroughly searched the film. This, however, did not reveal any articles. It is possible, therefore, that some articles were missed by failing to review film for all post-conviction dates. It is unlikely, however, that these articles would greatly impact the outcome of this analysis. For cases involving more than one trial and post-conviction phase, film was ordered for all dates. In all, 114 reels of microfilm were borrowed through ILL and approximately 55 hours were spent reviewing film.

These processes resulted in the collection of 1044 different newspaper accounts. The total cost of retrieving the articles was $1092. It is important to note that all editorials and letters to the editor were excluded from review. Only articles presented as "news" were included in this analysis. This was done to assure a consistent review of the ways in which local print media report these cases. I believed that including editorials or opinion pieces would have required a different kind of analysis.

CODING – CASE CHARACTERISTICS

Prior to coding beginning in earnest, two code sheets were developed. The variables were designed to gather information that related to the research questions and more. These sheets were modified as the coding progressed. The first code sheet was designed to measure the overall characteristics of the case (see Appendix C). It included 73 indicators, all of which could be coded objectively. These general case indicators included demographic information about the victim(s) and defendant, including race, gender, age, and victim/offender relationship. For the defendant, it also included information relating to the length of time on death row and prior felony and misdemeanor offenses. Code sheet one also included variables related to the characteristics of the crime. These variables include: charges against the defendant, location of the crime, weapons used, motive, aggravating factors, and injuries to the victim.

Code sheet one also contained variables relating to trials. These variables included: change of venue information, bail releases, public defenders, special prosecutors, the use of eyewitness testimony, codefendants, and types of evidence. It also included variables relating to bench versus jury trials and sentences. Code sheet one also measured post-conviction issues. This involved variables relating to the signing of death warrants, the reversing court, reasons for reversal, how the exoneration occurred, and post-reversal incarceration. Finally, code sheet one contained variables related to the identification of other suspects and lawsuits filed by the exonerated. All information relating to these variables were gleaned from the newspaper and review court opinions. When information was not provided about a specific variable, it was coded as "none reported" rather than missing.

CODING – THE ARTICLES

The second code sheet was specifically designed to explore death penalty legitimation techniques in the articles (see Appendix D).

Informed by Habermas' theory of legitimation crisis, I reasoned that I would need variables that could measure various legitimation techniques during the different phases of the case. First, however, it was necessary to determine article timing. In that vein, for each article I coded the story number, case number, and article timing. I divided timing by crime/investigation, arrest/pre-trial, trial, post-conviction, and exoneration. Crime/investigation included all reports of the crime prior to an arrest. Arrest/pre-trial stories included all reports the arrests and pre-trial events. Trial articles began with jury selection and ended with final sentencing. Retrials were also included as trial stories, as the new trials invalidated the others. Post-conviction articles included everything after final sentencing and prior to exoneration (excluding new trials). This involved all post-conviction appeals, case reversals, signing of death warrants, etc. Exoneration accounts included reports of court rulings that released a defendant, jury or bench verdicts that acquitted the defendant, the dropping of charges, and all post-exoneration stories. I coded the by-line of each article as none, staff reporter, or Associated Press (AP).

The first major issue I coded and counted was sources cited by the articles. The literature reviewed in the previous chapter suggests that legitimation relies on state sources. The sources counted included state, victim, defendant, court, accomplice, documents, politicians, professors, members of the community, and other. State sources included police, prosecutors, and state witnesses. Police sources were further identified as sheriff, detective/investigator, federal officer, police chief, other officer, police spokesperson, police report, prosecutor and the generic "police said." Prosecutor sourcing was identified as "in court," "out of court," or "other prosecutor." "In court" sourcing included any quotes or summaries of arguments, statements, and/or questioning of witnesses that occurred during the course of a formal proceeding. "Out of court" prosecutor sourcing included any statements attributed to a prosecutor that occurred external to official proceedings. "Other prosecutor" sources were those sources identified as a commonwealth's attorney, district attorney or prosecutor that was not affiliated with the defendant's case. State witnesses included anyone one who had or would testify on behalf of the state.

Victim sources included anyone identified as a friend, family member, and/or neighbor of the victim(s). Defense sources included the defendant and those identified as a defense attorney, friend, family member, neighbor of the defendant, or defense witness. Court sources were those identified as a judge, juror, or high court ruling. Alleged accomplices presented a dilemma. Due to the nature of the cases being explored, they have potential to be state witnesses who become defense witnesses. As a result, they were coded as "alleged accomplice for the state" and "alleged accomplice for the defense."

Document sources included any information attributed to an official report or other document. For example, medical examiner and laboratory reporters were counted as document sources, as were prison files. High court rulings and police reports were not included as documents. Sources identified as politicians involved any elected political official other than prosecutors and sheriffs. State Attorneys General, mayors, state and federal representatives, and senators were included in this category. Professors included any source identified as a college or university instructor or researcher. Other sources contained those not included in another category. For example, medical examiners and directors of non-profit organizations were coded as other sources. Finally, members of the community were those sources identified as someone other than the victims' or defendant's friend, family or neighbor who lived in the community. For example, sources identified as store owners and/or patrons were included in this category.

Following the identification of sources, I developed variables designed to reveal the presence of various legitimation techniques. As discussed previously, legitimation of the death penalty involves presenting it as being used for only the worst crimes, that threaten the moral order, and that it is fair and accurate. Additionally, I felt it was necessary to see if the underlying theme of defendant dangerousness was present. I attempted to create indicators that would elicit information that fit into each of these categories. First, to determine if the newspapers presented these as the "worst crimes," I developed two variables, "heinous crimes" and "sympathetic victims." I operationalized heinousness by reviewing the articles for mentions of blood, descriptions of the weapon(s), descriptions of the victims' injuries, and/or the use of "slash," "slit," or "slay." Further, mentions of "cold blooded," "heinous," vicious," or "violent" deaths were also identified as indicators of heinousness. Additionally, if the report revealed the number of wounds, defensive wounds, indicated that the victim was protecting another person, or mentioned gruesome photographs it was deemed as presenting the crime as particularly heinous.

The "worst crimes" category also involved a sympathetic victim variable. Several references to the victim were included in this category. For example, if the victim was referred to as "elderly," a "child," "helpless," and/or a good parent, spouse or worker this variable was coded as present. This variable also entailed references to the victim as a good member of the community, a student, religious, or if it described normative life experiences. It was also coded as a sympathetic victim reference if mention was made of the victim's hopes or dreams for the future, other recent tragedies suffered by the victim, or if it was reported that the victim complied with the demands of the assailant and was killed anyway. This variable also included references to the victim as a parent of a young child and other references. The "other" category included esteemed references like homecoming queen and honor student.

In an attempt to measure whether or not the crimes were presented as threatening the moral order, I developed a "public problems" variable. I coded for the presence of this variable if the article made reference to a quiet and/or middle-class neighborhood, referred to the rural or secluded location, or focused on community fear. Additionally, if a report indicated that neighbors were afraid or being cautious, reported that people are buying guns or other security devices, or if the article offered advice on self-protection it was coded for the presence of this variable. Reports of increased police presence in a community and pressure on the police to solve the crime were also identified as presenting the crime as a public problem.

The second variable in the moral order category was designed to determine if the police were presented as crime solvers. I reasoned that police are viewed as protectors of the moral order and if the articles functioned to legitimize the death penalty, the police would be presented as responding appropriately to the crime. The "crime solver" variable included descriptions of special investigative equipment, a technical investigation, or indicated that the police had spent long hours investigating the crime. Further, I coded for the presence of this variable if it reported that more police were assigned to the case, indicated that multiple agencies were investigating, mentioned that federal law enforcement agencies were participating, and/or indicated that specialized agents were utilized. I also included mentions of lab reports, gathering evidence, or looking for "clues." Additionally, mentions of "police priority," an indication of a quick arrest, or reference to police solving the crime were also indicators of this variable.

To determine if the death penalty was legitimized through its accuracy, I developed two variables on defendant guilt. The "guilt" variable included reports that the defendant, his/her car, or clothing had been identified in a line-up or photograph. It also involved statements that directly indicated the defendant was guilty or likely guilty. Reports of the defendant being near the scene or with the victim prior to death were also coded as presentations of guilt. Additionally, I coded this variable as present if an article reported that an alleged accomplice claimed the defendant's culpability, the defendant confessed, and/or failed a polygraph. Further, if the defendant was arrested quickly, if it was reported that the victim was afraid of the defendant, if the article indicated a lack of defendant emotion, or if the crime was part of a pattern of behavior, it was coded as presenting the defendant as guilty. Finally, if the relationship between the victim and defendant was presented in a way that indicated likely guilt (e.g., arguing spouses, victim afraid of defendant) I coded this variable present.

Second, I coded each article to determine if the defendant was presented as not guilty. This variable involved mentions of the defendant's alibi, reports of another suspect, and/or the failure of a witness to identify the defendant. This variable also included reports of problems with witness statements or capacity to testify, indicated that no evidence tied the defendant to the crime, or reported that there were no witnesses. Any description of evidence that alluded to the defendant's innocence was also an indicator of this variable.

To determine if the system was presented as "fair," I developed variables to determine how the articles presented the various aspects of the system. First, I developed one variable to determine if the newspapers attempted to educate the public about the functioning of the criminal justice system. This "how the system works" variable included descriptions of the pretrial process, sentence options, jury selection, and/or the appeals process. This variable was also present if the article defined: death eligibility, the purpose of a hearing, or another concept such as venue or motion. The articles were also coded to determine if the trials were presented as dramatic. The "drama" variable was considered present if the article mentioned a crowded courtroom or extra security. Reports of where the victim's and defendant's family were seated, as well as reports of the demeanor of family members, the defendant, and jurors were also indicative of drama. The "other" indicator involved reports of courtroom questioning or banter. Additionally, a variable was developed to measure whether or not the article presented the conviction as a failure of the system. This was indicated by anyone saying the system failed, outlining strong evidence of innocence, or a system functionary admitting a mistake.

The last major death penalty legitimation technique to be operationalized was the notion of defendant dangerousness. To this end, I developed two variables. First, I developed a "negative references" variable. This included general negative references about the defendant. For example, I coded for the presence of this variable if the article described the defendant as unemployed, a liar, an alcoholic, an outsider, a drug user, mentally ill, or a high school drop-out. Other references that were coded as being generally negative included reports that the defendant was incarcerated or denied bail, wearing shackles, handcuffs, and/or prison clothes. This variable was also coded as present if reference was made to intimidating characteristics of the defendant (such as large size), and/or negative demeanor in court (e.g. screaming at the jury or prosecutor). Finally, references were considered negative if the defendant was described as violent, had prior criminal convictions, or allegations of prior violence.

The other variable in the dangerousness category was "unsolved crimes." I sought to if determine the articles attempted to tie the defendant to other crimes. This variable included article themes, references to similarities between the charged crime and unsolved crimes, and reports that police agencies or officers believed unsolved crimes were connected to the charged crime. Additionally, it included mentions of police in one jurisdiction working with law enforcement in another, and even mentions of bodies being exhumed for further investigation.

I also sought to determine how the events that would lead to exoneration were presented in the post-conviction phase. The examination of appeals involved several variables. The first, was simply an effort to determine if the articles presented the appeals as too long. It included mentions of "lengthy appeals," or "years before execution." I also included a variable to determine if the defendant was presented as "fighting" the system with appeals. This involved an article tone that indicated the defendant was trying to avoid the inevitable, or appeals being presented in a negative way. An additional variable in this category was developed to determine if the appeals process was presented as necessary or positive. It was counted present if the article reported that anyone had a positive reaction to an appeal or indicated they were necessary. Finally, attempts to delegitimize appeals were measured by looking for statements from system functionaries that presented the appeal or reversal as legally invalid or a non-issue.

I further hypothesized that if the capital exonerations really presented a potential legitimation crisis the articles would contain relegitimation techniques. To this end, I reasoned that the primary attempts to relegitimate the system would involve presenting the exonerations as proof the system works, the exonerations would be presented as legal technicalities, and/or they would place blame. The "system works" variable included article themes and/or statements by functionaries or politicians to that end. The "technicality" variable included mentions of a "legal technicality" combined with descriptions of strong evidence of guilt. It also involved reports of close votes by review courts, quotes of dissenting opinions, and reports of excluded evidence impacting the state's ability to retry a defendant. The "blame" variable included any statements that alluded to the fact that someone or a particular institution was responsible for the wrongful conviction or the exoneration. I further categorized this variable in an attempt to determine who was being blamed: police, prosecutor, defendant, defense attorney, witness, judge, and/or review court.

I also sought to determine if the articles presented the exonerations as legitimate issues. This included indications that the system failed the defendant with the conviction, presented the defendant as not guilty, and/or outlined strong evidence of innocence. Assuming that not all the exonerations would be presented as legitimate issues, I developed a variable to determine if the article delegitimized the exoneration. This involved presentations of the exonerations as a technicalities, and/or the defendant as guilty.

Finally, I included several variables to determine if the articles mentioned certain things that did not necessarily fit into the other categories. For example, I included variables to count mentions of the race, age, and occupation of the victim and defendant. I counted death penalty mentions, listing of charges, and descriptions of the circumstances of the crime. I also reviewed the articles to see if they used phrases such as "death by electrocution," "the electric chair," or "death by lethal injection." Additionally, I counted articles that described efforts to change death penalty law, whether or not they reported how the victim was found, and the location and date of the crime.

Once the code sheets were developed and modified, I coded each article individually, in date order, by case. When coding was complete, I entered the results into two databases for the purpose of running frequency distributions. In addition to the coding efforts just described, I used narrative methods. Specifically, I maintained memo files. This coding technique involved summarizing each article and the dominant themes. The analytic memo writing efforts are further described below.

DATA ANALYSIS

The data for this research was analyzed using qualitative methods. Specifically, content analysis methods were used to determine what was reported, and narrative analysis was performed to determine how it was reported (Labov, 1997). The content analysis involved counts of sources, article timing, the presence of some words or phrases, by-lines, newspaper type, comparisons of story salience by victim and defendant demographics, and an examination of case characteristics. The narrative analysis worked to identify the presence and patterns of themes.

CONTENT ANALYSIS

Content analysis involves the analysis of text. This method has a long history and is widely used across disciplines. It is a nonreactive technique, meaning that the words or messages in the articles occurred without influence from the researcher. It is also unobtrusive (Webb, Campbell, Schwartz, Sechrist and Grove, 1981). The senders and receivers of these messages are unaware that it is being analyzed.

While content analysis can be utilized to make inferences about the sender of a message, the audience, or the message itself (Weber, 1990), this project focused only on the message. Each article was coded individually using systematic rules. The operationalization of variables was designed to increase the reliability and validity of the measures. Coding was conducted using manifest and latent analysis (Neuendorf, 2001). Berg (2001) argues that a blended approach should be used whenever possible. The manifest approach includes those elements that are visible on the surface of the message. It involves counts of words or phrases. The coding scheme contained variables designed to measure manifest content. These variables are outlined above and included the counts of sources and the presence of certain words or phrases. Specifically, actual counts were done of the sources referenced in each article while themes and certain words were sought for their presence in an article. It was deemed important to determine the frequency of themes across articles rather than within articles. This decision was made because the articles tended to have a general theme making a count within articles unnecessary.

Latent analysis was also utilized. It involves seeking underlying, implicit meaning in the text. I used this method to determine if a concept or theme was alluded to in the article. Latent coding of the articles sought the presence of a concept or theme rather than their frequencies. These variables were indicated by the presence of phrases, words, article themes, and other issues. The operationalization of latent variables was based on the presence of words, phrases, or issues that could have been counted. This was done in an effort to improve the reliability of the coding scheme. For example, as previously discussed, one latent variable attempts to measure whether or not an article presents the crime as particularly heinous. This variable was operationalized to include references to blood, the use of "slash" or "slit," and the use of "heinous" or "vicious." The presence of these words did not automatically indicate heinousness. The context in which they were used was an important factor. For example, if an article reported that someone developed a bloody nose during a court proceeding, the article was not coded for the presence of heinousness.

NARRATIVE ANALYSIS

Berg (2001, p. 241) posits that narrative analysis involves gleaning exhaustive "meaning of the text using specified rules and principles." Strauss (1987, p. 34) instructs researchers to form these principles and constructs based on "a combination of the researcher's scholarly knowledge and knowledge of the substantive field under study." The constructs I developed and used focused on legitimation efforts. Bishop (2003) argues that narratives frequently involve explanations for the actions of the participants. These explanations can also be viewed as legitimation efforts and served as the primary focus of this research. The narrative analysis of these cases involved the review of the articles to connect the text to context, form, and content. Narrative analysis involves the review of a chronological story. It often focuses on the sequencing of events, scripts, and the illumination of patterns of themes (Labov, 1997). This analysis utilized a chronological examination of each metastory to determine how the situation was presented when the script was disrupted.

The collection of newspapers from the discovery of a crime through exoneration facilitated the recognition of the cases as "metastories" with beginning, middles and ends. Metastories function "to generate a more inclusive perspective, and to expand the possibilities and range of debate" (Berdayes and Berdayes, 1998, p. 113). Viewing the cases as metastories contextualized each individual article. Quite simply, viewing the articles as metastories offers a clearer understand of the situation. Subjecting these metastories to narrative analysis enabled the exploration of assumptions underlying the text, and the examination of both linguistic and cultural resources utilized by the creators of the narratives (Berg, 2001). The examination of the subtleties of the narrative enabled a fuller understanding of the messages being sent.

In death penalty cases the script involves an expected sequence of events: crime, arrest, trial, conviction, death sentence, appeals, and execution. In these cases, the script was disrupted. The defendants were exonerated. Script disruptions can also be viewed as canonical events, which are unexpected elements that disrupt the expected progression of a situation (Bruner, 1990). The canonical events in these cases were the reversals, new evidence, and court orders that led to the subsequent exonerations. Bruner (1990) argues that reports of canonical events include an evaluative element that reveals the narrator's point of view. It involves presenting the script as good, bad, successful, tragic, or surprising. The articles were examined to determine if they contained manifest indicators of the messages about the death penalty. Essentially, these cases were narratively reviewed to determine how the local print media presented these cases before and after the canonical events.

Narrative analysis can also involve answering questions related to who, what, when, where, why, and how. The question of special importance here was "who." Specifically, the articles were reviewed to determine if the characterizations of the individuals who were the foci of the articles changed as the story changed. The articles were also examined to determine if they shared common themes. The themes reviewed were included in the content analysis coding process. They were also deduced through qualitative methods. Specifically, the examination of scripts, their disruptions, and themes was achieved through analytic memo writing and analytic comparison.

The first technique utilized was analytic memo writing, or at least a modified form of this method (Miles and Huberman, 1994). The traditional form involves a series of notes on thoughts and ideas about coding. Each theme or concept serves as the basis of an individual memo, which contains the researchers thoughts on the issue. For this project memo writing was modified. Instead of notes relating to "thoughts on coding," I used memos to summarize each article individually to facilitate the identification of specific themes. The summaries included the general content as well as notes regarding the presence of words, phrases, concepts, and themes. The articles were read in chronological order by case. The summaries included notes of characters, the issues, the sequence, and their structure. The articles were read to determine opposing issues and the characters associated with opposing viewpoints.

Analytic comparison is based on the work of John Stuart Mill (1843) and involves his method of agreement and method of difference approaches. The method of agreement focuses on similarities across cases and the method of difference seeks dissimilarities (Stinchcombe, 1968). While the two can be used independently, a double application results in a more thorough analysis. The primary factor in using analytic comparison is common outcomes. The nature of this study makes analytic comparison a logical choice. The themes and concepts important to this method were included as variables in the content analysis to provide a better idea of the frequency of their presence across cases and newspapers.

RELIABILITY AND VALIDITY

The goal of this project was to achieve a thorough understanding of the cases by examining how the local print media presented them. The use of content and narrative analysis made this a more thorough analysis. It strengthened the reliability and validity of the study and the chosen methods complemented one another. Three types of reliability are relevant to content analysis. They include reproducibility, accuracy, and stability (Weber, 1990). Reproducibility involves consistency between coders. While one person performed all coding for this project, two other researchers generously chose 30 articles at random and coded them. After comparing the results of this experiment, modifications were made to the variables, making for more consistent coding. The nature of this project allows the use of some variables that have been utilized by others, however, a majority were developed specifically for this study. Whenever possible, classification was consistent with other researchers. Particularly helpful in this regard were Chermak (1995a; 1998a; 1998b) and Paulsen (2003). The type of reliability most germane to this project was stability, or consistency in coding the same content more than once by the same coder (Weber, 1990). In an effort to be consistent and, therefore, reliable the articles were subject to repeated coding. Specifically, the articles were individually summarized. This was the first coding procedure. As the code sheet was developed and modified, twenty articles were randomly chosen and coded. The same articles were coded three times prior to coding beginning in earnest. Any discrepancies were reviewed and the coding was modified. This "practice" coding illuminated gray areas and facilitated the formulation of the final code sheet.

Validity is the extent to which an instrument measures what it is designed to measure (Cook and Campbell, 1979). There are two types of measurement validity that are particularly relevant to this study. First, face validity signifies that the indicator common sense definitions. Second, content validity is a type of face validity that seeks to assure that the full content of a definition is represented in a measure

(Carmines and Zeller, 1979). I believe that the constructed variables are sufficiently broad that they do contain the full content of their definitions and that the indicators measure the constructs. Each indicator of each variable was discussed with professional peers and modified until consensus was reached. Through these conversations, the indicators that I developed were narrowed or broadened as necessary. Further, some measures contain concurrent validity. For example, the variables relating to sources have been used by other researchers (see Chermak 1995a; 1998a; 1998b; Paulsen, 2003). In sum, I made every effort to assure the integrity, reliability and validity of the data and its analysis.

There is one problematic issue, however, that must be addressed. One portion of the content analysis involved an examination of the characteristics of the cases and their processing. The nature of the data presented a methodological concern for this portion of the analysis. The problem lies in treating reporters as data gatherers. The decision to report an issue was the choice of individual reporters and/or editors, as was the content of an article. Using that information to determine characteristics of the defendants' cases is problematic. The case characteristics, however, are important to understanding how wrongful convictions occur. They deserve attention. In an attempt to enhance the validity of these results, review court decisions were also used as a data source. This combination provided a relatively complete portrait of these cases. The limitations of using the newspaper accounts, however, should not be overlooked. The discussion of the findings of this portion of the analysis in Chapter Four assumes only that certain types of information was reported in some cases. Despite this weakness, the results of this segment of the analysis are important to achieving an understanding of the characteristics of wrongful capital convictions.

CHAPTER 4

The Cases in the News

Since the United States Supreme reinstated capital punishment in 1976 (see *Gregg v. Georgia*), 38 states have revised their death penalty statutes in an attempt to reduce arbitrariness. In most jurisdictions, these statutes require a bifurcated trial. Phase one includes the presentation of evidence and aggravating factors for the purpose of a finding of guilt or non-guilt. When the jury convicts, the penalty phase begins. During this phase the prosecution urges the jury to return a death verdict based on evidence of aggravating factors. The defense presents mitigation evidence and asks the jury to return a non-death verdict. The primary difference between the new and old statutes is the required presentation of aggravating and mitigating evidence. To be death eligible, a homicide must be accompanied by one or more aggravating factors. These are statutory and are different in each state. For example, Kentucky statutes list armed robbery and rape as aggravating factors. Mitigators are also statutory and vary by state. In Kentucky, diminished capacity due to drugs or alcohol is one of eight statutory mitigators. If the jury agrees that the aggravating factors outweigh the mitigating factors they can return a death verdict. When a death verdict is returned, appellate review is mandatory (Bohm, 2003).

Automatic appeals were a result of the *Gregg* (1976) ruling. Prior to *Furman* (1972), appeals were not mandatory and many death row inmates did not pursue them. In fact, Bohm (2003, p. 34) reports that "one-quarter of the prisoners executed" in the 1960s had no appeals at all, and two-thirds of executed defendants never had their cases reviewed by a federal court. The Supreme Court, in an attempt to achieve fairness in the process, ordered a mandatory review. Presently, most retentionist states automatically review both the conviction and sentence. The appeals process has been streamlined in recent years (Dieter, 1997). One important change in the appeals process since the *Gregg* (1976) ruling is that the Supreme Court will no longer consider issues raised for the first time pursuant to last-minute pleas for stays of execution, particularly when the claims could have been raised in prior habeas petitions (Bohm, 2003). This applies to claims of innocence. Specifically, in *Herrera v. Collins* (1993) the Supreme Court ruled that a claim of factual innocence based on new evidence is not grounds for granting an evidentiary hearing or a stay of execution. In short, the Justices ruled that it is not the Court's place to "correct errors of fact," even if the errors could lead to the execution of an innocent person (*Herrera v. Collins*, 1993). The claim must be accompanied by a procedural error.

In sum, death penalty law is quite complicated and varies by jurisdiction. When a wrongful conviction occurs, correcting the error can be extremely difficult. To some degree, the appeals process operates under the assumption that only legal or procedural errors, rather than factual errors, occur in the trial court system. This inquiry analyzes newspaper reports of the criminal justice system's processing of these cases. The cases were distinct in their facts, as they were in their experiences with the system. Before exploring the legitimation themes present in the reports, it is important to understand the characteristics of the cases, who spoke in the articles, and what factors most impacted story salience.

CASE CHARACTERISTICS

Recent research efforts have attempted to determine how people are wrongfully convicted of capital crimes. This section attempts to add to that undertaking by focusing on the specifics of the cases as they were summarized in court rulings and reported in the newspapers. Rather than focusing on the themes and tone of the articles, this section focuses on the content of what was reported about the processing of the cases.

DEFENDANT CHARACTERISTICS

Only one woman was included in this population, therefore other than the overrepresentation of males, defendant gender was not significant to the review of this data. This was anticipated because women represent only about one and one-half percent of the death row population (DPIC, 2003b). The cases were racially diverse, yet some discrepancies exist when making comparisons to the general population of death row inmates. White defendants were disproportionately represented in this population. Whites account for 42% of the death row inmates yet, 52% (n=15) of the cases in this population involved white defendants. African-Americans defendants were slightly underrepresented. They account for 46% of death row inmates, yet they accounted for 38% (n=11) of this population. The representation of Hispanics was on par with the death row population. They account for 10% of the general death row population and 10% (n=3) of this population.

The defendants' ages varied more than expected. The mean age was 31, with 65% (n=19) of the defendants being under 35 when arrested, 17% (n=5) were under 20, and 14% (n=4) were over 40. Fifty-five percent (n=16) of the population had been charged with or convicted of other felony offenses that were unrelated to the charges that sent them to death row. Additionally, 38% (n=11) had been charged or convicted of prior misdemeanor offenses.

The length of time spent on death row was calculated by determining the number of years each defendant was actually under a death sentence. The results of this analysis differ from those of Miller-Potter (2002). The mean years on death row was much shorter, and the discrepancies between minorities and non-minorities was smaller. As revealed in Table 4.1, minorities spent an average of one year longer on death row than non-minorities. Specifically, the mean number of years incarcerated for the overall population was 5.2. Whites spent an average of 4.7 years on death row. The average length of time on death row for African-Americans was 6.27. Hispanic defendants fared best in this regard. They spent an average of 3.7 years on death row. It is important to note that the duration of these cases was much longer than these numbers indicate.

The average time for the duration of all cases was 7.8 years. Only 28% (n=8) of all defendants were involved in cases that lasted longer than ten years. The length of time for minorities was slightly longer than the overall mean. The average number of years for the duration of cases with African-American defendants was 9. Again, Hispanic defendants experienced the shortest duration with 5 years. African-Americans defendants spent an average of 1.2 years longer waiting to be released than all defendants and 1.5 more years than whites.

TABLE 4.1   MEAN YEARS INCARCERATED

Defendant Race	Mean Years Duration	Mean Years on Death Row
All	7.8	5.2
White	7.4	4.7
African-American	9	6.27
Hispanic	5	3.7

VICTIM CHARACTERISTICS

The cases analyzed herein involved 39 victims. The mean victim age was 37, with the youngest victim being nine months and the oldest being 92. The number of victims per case was also reviewed. Seventy percent (n=20) of cases involved one victim. The analysis did reveal some racial disparity in this regard. In cases with white defendants, 30% (n=6) involved multiple victims, while only one case with an African-American defendant did. Of the nine cases that involved multiple victims, five were a married or cohabitating couple, two involved parents and children, and two involved acquaintances.

Female victims were disproportionately represented. Males are far more likely to be victims of homicide (BJS, 2003), yet in this population 66% (n=27) of the victims were female. Similar results were yielded by race. Even though whites are less likely than African-Americans to be victimized by homicide, 61% (n=25) of the victims in these cases were white. Only 17% (n=7) of the victims were African-American. It is important to note that in 22% (n=4) of cases the victim's race could not be gleaned from the data. It is likely, therefore, that white victims were even more disproportionately represented in this population of cases.

CRIME CHARACTERISTICS

The crimes that subsequently led to the wrongful convictions in these cases were diverse but several patterns were revealed. First, 45% (n=13) of the crimes occurred in urban areas, 38% (n=11) in rural areas, and 17% (n=5) in suburban areas. As revealed in Table 4.2, this pattern differed by race. White defendants were most likely to be charged with crimes that occurred in rural areas, while African-American and Hispanic defendants were far more likely to have been convicted of crimes in urban areas.

TABLE 4.2   CRIME LOCATION BY DEFENDANT RACE[1]

Defendant Race	Urban	Rural	Suburban	Victim Home	Public
White	33 (5)	53 (8)	13 (2)	73 (11)	13 (2)
African-American	55 (6)	27 (3)	18 (2)	36 (4)	55 (6)
Hispanic	67 (2)	0 (0)	33 (1)	67 (2)	33 (1)
Total	45 (13)	38 (11)	17 (5)	59 (17)	31 (9)

[1] These totals are not equal because some locations were unknown.

Second, and also presented in Table 4.2, a majority of the crimes took place in the victims' homes. In fact, 59% (n=17) occurred in the home of the victim(s), while 31% (n=9) were perpetrated in a public location, and seven percent (n=2) at the victim's workplace. This pattern also differed by defendant race. White defendants were charged far more often with crimes that occurred in the victims' homes, while minority defendants were charged with crimes that occurred in public. In one case the location of the victim's death was never determined.

Third, in 59% (n=17) of the cases the victim and defendant had some knowledge of one another prior to the crime. In 14% (n=4) of the cases the victim and defendant were spouses. In 10% (n=3) of cases they were neighbors, and in 35% (n=10) they were acquainted in some way. In 41% (n=12) of the cases the victim and defendant were strangers. This too had a racial dimension. Only 33% (n=5) of white defendants' cases involved stranger relationships. White defendants were charged with killing a spouse in 27% (n=4) of their cases, and 60% (n=6) involved some prior relationship between the victim and defendant. African-American defendants were charged with killing a stranger in 64% (n=7) of their cases, only 36% (n=4) involved acquaintances.

Fourth, the cases involving white defendants were intraracial while those with African-American defendants were evenly split. Only one case involved a white defendant and African-American victim. About one-half (n=6) of African-American defendants were charged with murdering a white victim. It is important to note at this point that the races of the victims in the cases of Hispanic defendants were not available for inclusion in this review.

The reported alleged motives for the crimes were diverse and included everything from property crimes to revenge. Robbery accounted for 28% (n=8) of motives in all cases, sexual assault 17% (n=5), burglary and drug related crimes accounted for 10% (n=3) each. Revenge and profit were cited as the motive in seven percent (n=2) of cases each, and "other" motives were present in 14% (n=4). These "other" motives included escaping arrest, child abuse, and an alleged racially motivated crime. The motives argued by the state in these cases were relatively consistent across races.

The reports of weapons used and injuries suffered by the victims indicated that 73 % (n=21) involved the use of one weapon. The most frequently used weapons were firearms, which were reportedly used in 52% (n=15) of the cases. Knives were reported in 35% (n=10) of case. Blunt objects, hands, and a car were the main weapons used in the remaining cases. Some differences were noted based on the race of the defendants. Cases with white defendants were far more likely to involve knives than those of minority defendants. Knives were used in · 47% (n=7) of cases with white defendants, 28% (n=4) with minorities, and only 27% (n=3) of cases with African-American defendants.

Multiple injuries to victims were reported in 48% (n=14) of all cases. Fifty-two percent (n=15) involved victims who were shot, 38% (n=11) were stabbed or cut, and 28% (n=8) were raped. The victims were beaten in 21% (n=6) of cases, and 14% (n=4) involved other injuries. These other injuries included being drowned, burned, and bitten. The number of types of injuries to the victims differed slightly by race of the defendants. In cases with white defendants 53% (n=8) of victims suffered multiple injuries. In cases with African-American defendants 45% (n=5) involved multiple types of injuries to the victims.

TRIAL CHARACTERISTICS

The reports and court rulings revealed that these 29 cases involved 51 trials. Fifty-five percent (n=16) of defendants had two trials, 38% (n=11) had one. One case had three criminal trials and one had five. These trials involved homicide and other charges. Aggravating factors are necessary for a case to be death eligible. The aggravating factors in three cases were not reported. For the remaining cases, 55% (n=16) included a single aggravating factor while 35% (n=10) involved multiple aggravators. Five cases with white defendants and three cases with African-American defendants involved multiple aggravators. One major difference was noted by race. White defendants were more likely to be charged with multiple homicides. Only one case with an African-American defendant involved a multiple homicide aggravator while 40% (n=6) of cases with white defendants were charged in this way.

I also reviewed the specific characteristics of the trials. For example, the newspaper accounts and court opinions revealed that 79% (n=23) of the cases were tried in the same county where the crime occurred. Additionally, juries were responsible for 100% (n=29) of the initial convictions, and for 62% (n=18) of the initial death verdicts. Thirty-five percent (n=10) of defendants were sentenced to death by judges. In one case this information was not reported.

I also paid special attention to the type of evidence used to convict the defendants. For example, four cases involved alleged accomplices who arranged plea bargains for their testimony. Eyewitness testimony was used against 28% (n=8) of the defendants, with 24% (n=7) involving an eyewitness identification of the defendant at or near the scene. Additionally, scientific evidence was remarkably absent from these cases. In fact, 65% (n=19) of cases involved no scientific evidence. In the cases that contained testimony they involved glass fragments, bite marks, DNA, blood type matches, hair, fiber evidence, footprints, and fingerprints. The two other primary forms of evidence used to convict these defendants were circumstantial and confession evidence. Defendants in 48% (n=14) of the cases were largely convicted by circumstantial evidence, and 38% (n=11) were confronted by confession evidence. Jailhouse informants were the primary sources of confessions in 6 cases. The police were the alleged recipients of confessions in 5 cases. Two cases involved multiple alleged confessions to others. In sum, the most frequent type of evidence in all cases was circumstantial. Scientific evidence was rare but was the second most frequently used.

EXONERATION CHARACTERISTICS

I also recorded the information reported about the exonerations. The defendants in this population spent a combined 227 years under charges and a combined 151 years on death row. The reversing courts were overwhelmingly state supreme courts. They were responsible for 66% (n=19) of the reversals. Other state appeals courts reversed 17% (n=5), and trial courts reversed 10% (n=3). Two cases did not involve reversals. In one case the prosecutor agreed to a retrial after DNA evidence indicated a man who was incarcerated for a similar crime had actually committed the two rapes and homicides. The prosecutor later dropped the charges. The second case involved a defendant who died of cancer on death row.

The reasons for reversal cited by courts were diverse. Several of the cases involved more than one reason for reversal, which is common in these cases and in agreement with the research of Miller-Potter (2003). The most common reason for reversal was prosecutorial misconduct, it was cited by review courts in 28% (n=8) of cases. Judicial error was involved in 24% (n=7) of cases. The remaining cases were reversed on lack of evidence, ineffective counsel and testimony issues. Each of these reasons were cited in 10% (n=3) of cases.

The review court orders for new trials and even orders of release did not automatically free the defendants. In fact, 90% (n=26) of the defendants were incarcerated after the reversals in their cases. Only two defendants were released immediately. In most of these cases the defendants were held in jail while awaiting retrials. In cases that the involved court ordered releases the prosecutors appealed the decision. Court ordered releases were involved in only two cases. Bench trial acquittals were responsible for three of the exonerations. Jury trial acquittals led to 38% (n=11) and dropping of charges led to 41% (n=12) of the releases.

The exonerations of these defendants rarely led to charges being pursued against another suspect. Only 17% (n=5) of the cases involved charges against another suspect. This, however, does not accurately reflect what occurred. Two of the cases that involved charges against other suspects were actually the alleged accomplices of the defendants. In both cases post-conviction investigations revealed that the defendants were framed by those who committed the crimes, and they both involved plea arrangements for lesser sentences by the likely offenders. A more accurate analysis of the status of these cases indicates that only 10% (n=3) of the exonerations led to charges being filed against other suspects. By December 31, 2002 only two cases involved convictions of other suspects. In one case the other suspect received the death penalty (Godfrey, 2001) and in the other the suspect received life without the possibility of parole (Daley, 2000).

The ordeals of these defendants led to little compensation from the state. Only 28% (n=8) of defendants were reported to have filed lawsuits seeking monetary compensation. Unfortunately, a majority of these cases were not resolved by the end of the review period. Most lawsuits were dismissed, though a few states sought to pass legislation designed to provide compensation for the wrongfully convicted. In any event, the defendants were rarely compensated for the years they spent wrongfully confined on death rows. Three of the defendants (10%) faced other unrelated charges upon their releases. In one case, the defendant had escaped from a work release program in another state. He spent 14 years in prison, eight of them on death row and the prosecutor in his case contacted a state's attorney in another state to notify him of the defendant's release. When he was released from homicide charges he was extradited to the other state to complete his sentence (Hill, 1999).

NEWSPAPER COVERAGE

The cases in this population tended to be relatively high profile and received a great deal of coverage. The newspapers that reported on these cases were regional dailies, local dailies, and weekly papers (see Appendix B). As revealed in Table 4.3, regional papers accounted for 58% (n=610) of the articles, while local dailies and weeklies were responsible for 3%1 (n=327), and 10% (n=107) respectively. Staff reporters' by-lines appeared on 87% (n=905) of all articles.

TABLE 4.3   BY-LINES BY NEWSPAPER TYPE

By-line	Regional	Daily	Weekly	Totals
Staff	84 (510)	92 (300)	89 (95)	87 (905)
None	12 (76)	7 (23)	11 (12)	10 (111)
AP	4 (24)	1 (4)	0 (0)	3 (28)
Totals	100 (610)	100 (327)	100 (107)	100 (1044)

Only 11% (n=111) of the articles had no by-line and only three percent (n=28) were attributed to wire or Associated Press (AP) writers. As presented in Table 4.3, all papers relied heavily on staff writers to cover the stories, though articles from regional papers were slightly less likely to contain staff by-lines. The reliance on staff writers is indicative of the importance of these stories. Most of the newspapers followed the metastories through their duration. Some patterns were, however, revealed regarding the duration of coverage.

ARTICLE TIMING

The first pattern found in the articles was that the articles were clustered in waves. These waves were directly related to the stages of the criminal justice process and contained very distinct themes that were discernable from the data. The beginning of each wave was indicated by shifts in news themes, article focus, and the type of information presented, not just a progression through the system. As presented in Table 4.4, five waves were recognized from the data, and the articles were somewhat evenly divided across waves. Wave one reports appeared after the crime, but prior to arrest. It accounted for 11% (n=119) of the articles. Articles in wave one focused on the details of the crimes and the actions of the police. The victims and the investigating police agencies were the main characters. Accounts of the crimes tended to depend heavily on state sources, which were supplemented by victim and community sources. These accounts tended to present the victims as sympathetic and the crimes as public problems.

Wave two reports began with the arrest of the individual who would ultimately be exonerated. It accounted for 16% (n=173) of the articles. Wave two reports tended to focus on victims, defendants, and the crimes. These accounts tended to present the victims as sympathetic, the crimes as heinous, and the defendants as not only guilty of the crimes, but as bad people. The articles relied on state sources, with defense and court sources making rare appearances.

TABLE 4.4 ARTICLES BY WAVE AND PHASE OF THE CASE

Wave	Case Phase	Articles
1	Crime Reported	11 (119)
2	Arrest/Pre-trial	17 (173)
3	Trial	26 (266)
4	Post-Conviction	24 (255)
5	Exoneration	22 (231)

Wave three reports began with jury selection and ended with final sentencing. It accounted for 25% (n=266) of the articles. Wave three reports tended to focus on the state's attempts to prove the defendants' guilt at trials. The defendants were the main characters. The victims were still important characters, but were no longer the primary focus of the metastory. The articles still relied heavily on state sources though defense sources finally appeared in a majority of stories. Heinous representations increased in wave three, as did presentations of the defendants' guilt. Fewer articles presented the victims as sympathetic characters and the death penalty became a key issue.

Wave four reports included all post-sentencing issues. Essentially, this wave began with the defendant arriving on death row. It included all reports of appeals, signing of death warrants, and pre-retrial accounts. It accounted for 24% (n=255) of the articles. Wave four reports were prompted by a variety of issues. These most commonly included the discovery of new evidence, questions about trial fairness, filing of appeals, and reversals. Other, less frequent issues included the signing of death warrants, death row status reports, and infamous crimes. Wave four marked the beginning of the canonical events. These script changes greatly impacted the way information was presented. Patterns were recognized from the data, but the issues were so diverse that for the first time in the metastories, the articles assumed individual character. The primary focus of each article depended heavily on what prompted the story.

The most significant change in wave four accounts was that they began to question the defendants' guilt. The defendants were the main characters and the victims became minor characters. The gap between state and defense sources was narrowed in wave four, which had an enormous impact on both the content and tone of the accounts. The percentages of articles containing heinous representations and indicators of the defendants' guilt both decreased. Sympathetic depictions of the victims decreased considerably and the integrity of the state's case received more attention.

Wave five reports appeared after retrial acquittals, court ordered releases, or dropping of charges. In other words, wave five included all exoneration reports. It accounted for 22% (n=231) of the articles. Wave five reports focused on the metastory in its totality. The two major foci of wave five accounts were questions relating to "how did this happen?" and the relegitimation of capital punishment. Wave five accounts depended heavily on state sources, though defense sources were present in a majority of articles. The crimes and victims were all but forgotten in these accounts, with both receiving very little attention.

STORY SALIENCE

The discovery of the crimes was the catalysts for the coverage in 24 cases. Coverage in two cases began with the arrests of the defendants, in one case it began with the trial, and in one case coverage began only when exoneration was imminent. The continuation of coverage throughout the metastory, and the frequency of reports were impacted by the number of victims, victim race and age, crime location, and defendant race.

The mean number of articles per case was 36. Cases involving victims under 18 had the highest mean. These cases averaged 62 articles while those involving adult victims averaged 29. Crimes involving multiple victims averaged 48 articles while those with single victims averaged 30. Cases with white victims received more attention than those with African-American victims. The mean for cases with white victims was 39. Cases with African-American victims averaged 32. One case had a heavy impact on the mean for African-American victims. It involved a 17 year-old high school student who was apparently abducted from school. There was a four year gap between the crime and the arrest of the defendant. During that gap, the newspaper ran numerous articles that focused on the investigation. When that case is removed, the mean number of articles for African-American victims was 16.

Other factors also impacted the average number of articles per case. Crimes that occurred in victims' homes received more attention than others. These cases averaged 38 articles per case, while those that occurred in public locations averaged 31. Since the newspapers reported the type of area in which the crimes occurred, or it was possible to glean this information from the reports, I was able to determine that crimes in suburban locations received more coverage than others. Suburban crimes resulted in a mean of 48 articles. Cases that occurred in rural locations averaged 37 articles per case, while those in urban locations averaged 29. Additionally, the defendant's race also impacted local newspaper coverage of the cases. White defendants' cases averaged 48 articles, while those with African-American and Hispanic defendants averaged only 22.

SOURCES

The articles relied heavily on state sources. State sources included police officers, prosecutors, and reports from state agencies. As shown in Table 4.5, at least one state source was referred to in 71% (n=742) of the reports. Prosecutors were the primary state source cited, they appeared in 41% (n=424) of the articles. Police sources were mentioned in 28% (n=288). The type of police source varied considerably. Sheriffs were cited in only five percent (n=56), detectives/investigators in nine percent (n=91), chiefs in two and one-half percent (n-26), other officers in seven percent (n=72), and "police said" was used in 10% (n=108). Additionally, individuals who testified on behalf of the state were cited in 20% (n=209) of all articles.

Defense and court sources appeared far less frequently than state sources. At least one defense source was referred to in 46% (n=478) of the articles. Defense attorneys were the principal defense source, they were cited in 35% (n=368) of the articles. Defendant family and defense witness sources were mentioned in only seven percent (n=74) each. The defendants were cited as sources in 17% (n=176) of all articles. Court sources included judges, jurors, and high court rulings. They were mentioned in 22% (n=235) of all accounts. Judges were cited in 13% (n=137) of all articles, jurors in only three percent (n=32), and court rulings in eight percent (n=81). Victim sources included friends, family and neighbors of the victims. They were mentioned in 14% (n=150). Community members were cited in only four percent (n=43), and "other" sources were mentioned in 22% (n=233).

The newspaper articles analyzed herein clearly relied on state sources throughout the metastories. Defense and court sources were important, but were mentioned far less frequently. Victim and community sources were infrequent. These patterns are important, but these facts alone do not adequately reveal the impact these sources had on the tone, content, and themes in the articles throughout the metastories. This is revealed only by a description of the source changes by wave.

The individuals quoted or cited in wave one accounts were overwhelmingly state sources. As indicated in Table 4.5, at least one state source was cited in 84% (n=100) of wave one articles. These accounts depended heavily on police sources, which accounted for a majority of state sources in wave one. Police sources were cited at least once in 80% (n=95) of wave one accounts. Police officers whose names were provided but were not identified as detectives or spokespersons were sources in 35% (n=41) of articles. The generic "police said" was present in 33% (n=39), and detectives were cited in 26% (n=31) of wave one articles. Less than two percent (n=2) of wave one accounts named "police reports" as sources, indicating that the individuals who gathered information for these reports sought information directly from the police.

Wave one accounts also involved victim and community sources. Victim sources were cited in 31% (n=37) of wave one articles. A family member of the victim was a source in 19% (n=22) of wave one accounts. Victim friends and neighbors accounted for 13% (n=16) and 14% (n=17) respectively. Community members were named sources in 19% (n=23) percent of wave one accounts.

TABLE 4.5   SOURCES BY WAVE

	All	Crime	Arrest	Trial	Post-conviction	Exoneration
State	71	81	81	74	67	58
Sources	(739)	(100)	(140)	(198)	(171)	(133)
Defense	46	3	34	52	63	58
Sources	(478)	(3)	(59)	(139)	(144)	(133)
	41	4	41	46	41	41
Prosecutor	(424)	(5)	(71)	(121)	(131)	(96)
	28	80	51	11	12	19
Police	(288)	(95)	(89)	(29)	(32)	(43)
Defense	35	1	25	42	49	38
Attys	(368)	(1)	(44)	(111)	(124)	(88)

Reports in wave two continued to rely on state sources for information. At least one state source was cited in 81% (n=140) of wave two accounts. Again, police sources were the most frequent with 51% (n=89) of articles containing at least one police source. Prosecutors began to appear in the stories with 41% (n=71) of articles containing at least one prosecutor source. Defense attorneys were cited in 25% (n=44) of articles and judges only in 14.5% (n=25).

Wave three reports continued to rely on state sources for information. At least one state source was cited in 74% (n=198) of wave three articles. For the first time in the metastory prosecutors, not police, were the primary state source. Prosecutors were cited in 46% (n=121) of articles while police sources were only cited in 11% (n=29). Defense attorneys were cited in 42% (n=111) of articles and judges only in 14% (n=25). Defendants were cited in 21% (n=57) of wave three accounts.

The presence of defense attorney and defendant sources was not indicative of a balanced representation. These articles focused on the trials of these defendants. The content of the stories primarily revolved around the state's attempts to prove their guilt. The newspapers did not present a balanced portrait of both sides. This is revealed through witness sources. Wave three accounts included far more witness sources than any other wave. It is significant that 47% (n=124) of the articles cited at least one state witness source while only 17% (n=40) cited a defense witness source. The accounts of these criminal trials overwhelmingly focused on the state's case and presented them as stronger than the defendant's case. For example, when jury selection began in Andrew Golden's trial, the *Tampa Tribune* reported that the prosecutor "plans to prove" a serious of incriminating issues while the defense would "point out" others (Foushee, 1991a).

State sources appeared in a majority of wave four reports, though defense sources received almost as much attention. At least one state source was cited in 67% (n=171) of wave four articles. Prosecutors continued to be the primary state source. They were cited in 51% (n=131) of articles. Police sources were cited in only 12% (n=32). Defense sources became an important source of information in wave four articles, with 56% (n=144) containing at least one defense source. Defense attorneys were cited in 48% (n=125) of articles. Defendants were cited in 16% (n=41) of wave four accounts, and court sources were cited in 37% (n=95) percent.

For the first time in the metastories, wave five accounts provided equitable space to defense and state sources. In fact, defense sources peaked, they were mentioned in 58% (n=133) of wave five accounts. Defense attorneys appeared in 38% (n=88) of articles and defendants were cited in 30% (n=69). State sources appeared in 58% (n=133) of wave five articles. Prosecutors continued to be the primary state source in wave five accounts. They were cited in 41% (n=96) of articles. Politicians were mentioned as sources in 17% (n=39) of wave five accounts. Court sources were cited in 25% (n=57). Police officers were named in 18% (n=43).

The examination by wave indicates that state sources were the most frequent regardless of wave, though the primary state source changed. In waves one and two police were the main sources of information. They were largely absent until wave five when they reentered. Prosecutors were consistently relied on as primary sources of information in waves three, four, and five. The nature of the information presented changed, however. In wave three, quotes and information described as originating with prosecutors was predominately identified as in court activity. In waves four and five, statements and information from prosecutors originated outside the courtroom. They were primarily reactions to changes in the case.

While defense sources never surpassed state sources, they did finally match state sources in wave five. There were, however, changes in the nature and context of the information defense sources provided. They were absent from wave one for an obvious reason, there was no defendant. In wave two defense sources began to appear, but were largely absent. A majority of wave three accounts included defense sources, as with prosecutors, these were primarily in court statements. This is indicative of the fact that the articles in wave three reported the activities of the trials and did little exploration beyond what occurred in the courtrooms. Defense sources increased in wave four and peaked in wave five. This was due to the canonical events. When the state faced serious questions about the convictions, defense sources appeared more frequently in the articles. Essentially, the reports began to present alternate explanations and questions about the states' cases that were often raised by defense attorneys. Additionally, defendants as sources of information increased in wave four and peaked in wave five.

OVERVIEW

Despite the small population size, the results of this portion of the analysis lend some support to other research that has been conducted sources in crime stories and story salience. Story salience was impacted by victim and offender characteristics. Specifically, cases involving white victims received more coverage than those with minority victims. These results are similar to that of Johnstone, Hawkins, and Michener (1994), Chermak (1998a), Wilbanks (1984); Pritchard and Hughes (1997), and Sorenson, Manz, and Berk, (1998) among others. Additionally, and similar to Duwe (2000), the cases with child and multiple victims received more coverage than other cases. Essentially, this research supports the notion that the media focuses on the sensational. Likewise, the cases with white defendants were covered more extensively than those involving minorities, which supports the findings of Chermak (1998b) and Paulsen (2003).

Additionally, these newspapers also relied heavily on state sources for information. This analysis supports the research of Sigal (1973), Chermak (1995a; 1995b), and Haney and Greene (2004) among others, who each revealed that more than half of all sources in articles about crime are police, prosecutors, or other representatives of the state. These newspapers' dependence on state sources was consistent regardless of geography, newspaper size, or wave. During every stage of the case, the reports focused on the presentation of the state's message. The only exception to this was wave five. The exoneration reports included information from defense sources to present a more balanced effort. Most importantly, however, is that the content of what was reported was impacted by the absence of defense sources and the reliance on state sources for information.

CHAPTER 5

Legitimizing the Death Penalty

The reports of crimes, investigations, arrests, and trials of these defendants contained very distinct patterns that functioned to legitimize the ultimate punishment. These crimes were presented as the "worst" cases thus making them eligible for capital punishment. The victims were presented as positive forces and the defendants were presented as not only bad people, but as threats to the moral order.

THE CRIMES

The crimes were a significant part of the metastories. They were the catalysts for all subsequent events and received a great deal of attention. The crimes were presented as particularly heinous events in 43% (n=445) of all articles. The date of the crime was reported in 71% (n=740) of articles, the motive in 33% (n=344), and the location in 68% (n=709). The crimes were presented as public problems in 16% (n=162) of all articles. The primary issue surrounding the presentations of the crimes was the degree of heinousness indicated by the articles.

The data revealed that heinous representations were achieved through descriptions of the victims' injuries and the use of certain words to describe those injuries. The presence of the descriptions and use of words like "slay," "slash," and "slit" resulted in a tone that indicated the crime was heinous. As with all other themes in the metastories, the presentations of the crimes changed as the stories changed. As indicated by Table 5.1, the information reported about the crimes fluctuated by wave. These shifts provide a logical organization to the discussion of the articles' presentations of crimes.

Wave one accounts provided generic information on the crime and tended to focus on presenting the situation as a public problem. The generic information included reports of the date and location of the crime. In wave one, 88% (n=105) of articles reported the date the crime occurred or the date the victim was noticed as missing. The location of the crime was reported in 84% (n=100) of wave one articles, and how the victim was found was reported in 51% (n=43). Interestingly, the state's theory of motive was presented in 17% (n=20) of articles and a detailed description of the confrontation between the victim and offender was provided in 18.5% (n=22).

Only 40% (n=48) of articles presented the crimes as particularly heinous. This is likely due to details of the cause of death being withheld by police and/or unknown prior to autopsy results. The cases in which these details were known, however, did allow for representations of heinousness. For example, in May, 1985 in Fayetteville, North Carolina a woman and two of her children were found murdered. When autopsy results were released, the following description was reported:

> Kathryn Eastburn was sexually assaulted before she and two of her daughters were slain last week in their home... Autopsies revealed they died of multiple stab wounds in the chest area and their throats had been slashed, authorities said. (Krisher, 1985a).

Importantly, this information was attributed to "authorities," the nature of the information did not require a specific source. Further, while the reports were presenting factual information, it was the words they used that indicated that it was a particularly heinous crime. When police hope to solve "the grisly June 1994 slayings" in which "Bonnie Dryfuse had been stabbed 28 times; Jacqueline, 14 times; Heather, 16 times; and Stephanie six times" (Bucsko, 1996) it sent a message to the reader that the crime was particularly brutal, heinous and deserving of the harshest punishment.

Wave one accounts also presented the crimes as being public problems. This was achieved through story focus and the underlying tone of the articles. When the articles focused on community fear, neighbors buying guns and other self-protection devices, or the police offered advice on self-protection, it sent a message to the reader that the situation was a community problem. These themes were present in

55.5% (n=66) of wave one articles. Public problem representations primarily occurred in cases that involved crimes in the home that appeared to be perpetrated by a stranger. The predominant theme in these articles was the fear felt by neighbors. This was particularly true in cases involving elderly victims. For example, when a second elderly woman was found murdered "less than a block away on the same street" from a previous murder the paper reported "that revelation has set area residents turning on outside lights, digging guns from closets and in some cases talking about moving" (Shell, 1987a). This theme continued until an arrest was made, with police "trying to calm neighborhood fears that more attacks are inevitable" (Shell, 1987b). The focus on fear among elderly residents of a neighborhood sent the message that they should be concerned for their safety.

TABLE 5.1   CRIME INFORMATION REPORTED BY WAVE

	Crime	Arrest	Trial	Post-conviction	Exoneration	All Waves
Date	88 (105)	84 (145)	89 (238)	65 (166)	37 (86)	71 (740)
Location	84 (100)	82 (141)	83 (222)	59 (150)	41 (96)	68 (709)
Motive	17 (20)	49 (84)	44 (119)	35 (89)	14 (32)	33 (344)
Victim found	51 (43)	30 (51)	23 (62)	13 (34)	10 (23)	21 (221)

Other articles presented the crime as a concern for the larger community. When the murder of an elderly man made "1993 the deadliest year on record" the report focused on a city-wide fear. It reported that "sales of personal protection items, whether Mace or guns, have increased dramatically in the wake of the last two murder and mayhem-filled weeks" (Baggs, 1993). A focus on the fear of the larger community was primarily present in cases in which the crime occurred in public. These cases, however, were all presented as stranger crimes. For example, when three young women were missing in Omaha, Nebraska, articles highlighted the fear felt by other young women. One article focused solely on self-protection. It reported that "a would-be attacker is looking for prey" and offered a list of "precautions

that experts suggest for women" (Taylor, 1992). The message sent by
these reports is one of fear. They functioned to present these crimes as
a problem for the neighborhood and the larger community (Altheide,
2002).

Wave two accounts focused on the heinous nature of the crimes
and the state's theories of them. Generic details were also provided.
The location of the crime was reported in 81.5% (n=141) of wave two
articles and the date was reported in 84% (n=145). Details of the
encounter were slightly more likely to appear in wave two articles with
30% (n=51) of articles reporting a detailed description of the crime and
30% (n=51) reporting how the victim was found. A motive was
reported in 49% (n=84) of articles, and 64.2% (n=111) presented the
crimes as particularly heinous. Interestingly, only 18% (n=31) of
articles continued to present the crime as a public problem.

What is especially significant about the increase in heinous
presentations between waves one and two is that they are tied to the
presentation of a guilty defendant. As revealed in Table 5.2, the
descriptions of the crimes changed and included more heinous
references when the defendant was arrested and presented as guilty. For
example, prior to the arrest of Frank Lee Smith in Broward County,
Florida the paper reported that the assailant "struck her with a sharp
weapon and sexually assaulted her" (Springer, 1985). After Smith's
arrest, it was reported that the victim's mother "found her daughter
crumpled on the floor, her face covered with blood from a head injury
and a piece of cloth tied tightly around her neck, cutting off her breath"
(Connelly, 1985a). In the case of Robert Miller, the paper reported that
one victim was "asphyxiated" and the other was "the apparent victim of
a beating" (Thornton and Ellis, 1986). After his arrest, Miller was
accused of "raping then strangling or smothering" the victims and of
using "a knife in the sexual assault" (*Daily Oklahoman*, 1987c).

The presentation of the crimes as public problems decreased
considerably with the arrests of the defendants. While presenting the
crimes in this way was done sporadically in wave two, the cases in
which it continued had some interesting characteristics. Only eight
cases contained articles with public problems themes in wave two, but
seven of them involved crimes directed at children or the elderly. The
only exception to this involved a stranger homicide that occurred in a

public location. In all the articles that continued the public problems themes, the crimes were presented as part of patterns.

TABLE 5.2 ARTICLE THEME BY WAVE

Theme	Crime	Arrest	Trial	Post-conviction	Exoneration	All Waves
Heinous Crime	40 (48)	64 (111)	70 (187)	26 (66)	14 (33)	43 (445)
Sympathetic Victim	61 (72)	61 (106)	46 (124)	32 (82)	21 (48)	43 (445)
Guilty Defendant	5 (6)	65 (113)	70 (187)	53 (136)	28 (63)	45 (473)
Bad Defendant	4 (5)	46 (80)	39 (104)	24 (60)	17 (40)	28 (289)
Public Problems	56 (66)	18 (31)	9 (24)	8 (20)	3 (8)	15 (162)
Police Crime Solvers	67 (80)	35 (61)	7 (20)	3 (8)	4 (9)	17 (178)

These articles described community fears using statements from neighbors, reports of gun sales, and reports of many "for sale" signs posted on lawns. Statements that indicated the fears were justified tended to follow these descriptors. This technique was exemplified by a report that followed the arrest of Robert Miller. Under the headline "Arrest Fails to Calm Fears in Military Park," neighbors were quoted as being "scared to death." For "several elderly widowed women, life will never be the same." They were "afraid to come outside, especially at night" since the murders. The article then quoted the prosecutor who assured "the public" that "this man is in custody and the danger is over." This was followed by a quote from an elderly woman who said "but there's always someone to take his place." The next sentence was: "recent crimes in the area would seem to support her belief." The article then goes on to list recent rapes and robberies in the area (Thornton, 1987b).

The same pattern was present in other reports. They all contained references to community fears, a statement by an official attempting to assuage those fears, and then reports of increased criminality. The people interviewed, tended to have characteristics similar to the victim(s). Consider the article just described. The reporter specifically wrote about the fact that "elderly widowed women" were afraid. The victims in this case were two elderly, widowed women who lived alone. What the article did not do was indicate whether the residents were afraid before the murders. It assumed that the murders were the catalyst for the fears.

Wave three accounts presented the crimes as heinous and overwhelmingly described the state's theories of them. The reports continued to provide basic information about the crimes. The location of the crime was reported in 83% (n=222) of the articles and the date was reported in 89% (n=238). Graphic details of the crime appeared in 30% (n=81) but only 23% (n=62) reported how the victim was found. Oddly, the state's theory of motive was reported less often in wave three accounts. It was reported in only 44% (n=119) of articles. Heinous representations, however, peaked in wave three, with 70% (n=187) of articles presenting the crimes as particularly heinous. This is commonsensical, at this point in the metastories more information was known about the crimes.

Wave three included all accounts of trials and often included testimony from medical examiners who offered detailed descriptions of the victims' injuries. The standard descriptions of the crimes often changed as a result of trial testimony. For example, prior to Randall Padgett's trial the crime was described as a "stabbing death and rape" (*Huntsville Times*, 1990) or the report indicated the victim died of "numerous stab wounds" (Nichols, 1992a). Upon reporting the opening arguments of the trial, it was reported that "the woman was stabbed more than 40 times and that she had been raped after the assault" (Nichols, 1992b). After the medical examiner's testimony the victim's injuries were described as:

> approximately 46 sharp force injuries... with six in the head and neck area, 13 in the chest and abdomen area, four in the right arm and hand and 22 in the left arm and hand.... Prior testimony indicated that Mrs. Padgett may have been raped after she was unconscious or dead (Nichols, 1992c).

In the case of Gary Gauger, the victims were described as being "stabbed to death" in pretrial accounts (Holmes, 1993). During the trial, however, the reports were quite gruesome. In a report that described the testimony of the forensic pathologist the following descriptions were reported:

> Jurors viewed photos of the couple's bloody remains and heard discussion about precisely how they were slain... By the end, the viciousness of the crimes was underscored: The photos showed, for instance, that the throats of Morris Gauger, 74, and his wife Ruth, 70, had been slashed all the way to their spinal columns.
>
> The attack against Ruth Gauger... was slightly more vicious than that against her husband. While Morris Gauger's throat was deeply slashed twice, his wife's was slit three times, from the left side of her neck all the way to her right ear. (McRoberts, 1993a).

Prior to Clarence Dexter's trial, his wife's death was described as resulting from the fact that she "had been shot with a .32-caliber semiautomatic pistol" (Kuhl, 1990). During the first trial, which ended in a mistrial, it was reported that the victim "had been shot at least four times with a .32-caliber semiautomatic pistol and also was beaten repeatedly with a hammer" (Kuhl, 1991a). The second trial witnessed a progression to a more heinous account. When the judge overrode the jury and handed down a death verdict, it was reported that "Dexter shot his wife four times and later beat her with a hammer when he saw she hadn't died from the gunshots" (Kuhl, 1991b). The judge described the crime as "outrageous and wantonly vile, horrible and inhumane... and as unreasonably brutal" (Kuhl, 1991b). Heinous presentations did not work alone to achieve a tone that legitimized the death penalty. The papers also presented the victims as sympathetic and the defendants as bad people.

THE VICTIMS

The victims and defendants were the main characters in the metastories. The victims were presented as sympathetic characters while the defendants were presented as bad people. In the early waves a dichotomous presentation was prominent. The victims were good people who encountered an evil person. The defendants were portrayed in a generally negative way. Rarely did the early articles mention positive defendant characteristics, and negative descriptions of the victims were even more infrequent.

As revealed in Table 5.3, the victims were the main characters in wave one accounts though this focus changed as the story progressed. These reports provided demographic information on the victims and presented them as particularly sympathetic, undeserving individuals. The victim's age was reported in 91% (n=108) of articles and the victim's name was reported in 98% (n=117). None of the wave one accounts reported the victim's race, while 55% (n=65) reported the victim's job. None of the articles in wave one made any negative references to the victim, instead, 61% (n=72) presented the victims as sympathetic.

Sympathetic victim references revolved around presenting them as good people who had positive, normative life experiences disrupted by violence. For example, when Michael Gerardi was killed during a robbery outside a French Quarter restaurant, the wave one accounts characterized him as a "hard worker. Great guy. Sweet romantic." The reports of his good nature, and therefore, his sympathetic character, were compounded by the "storybook promise" that "had a horror-show ending. Three armed robbers. A gunshot to the head" (Cooper and Boyd, 1995). The adult victims were consistently presented in wave one accounts as good parents, loving people, and/or good community members.

TABLE 5.3   VICTIM INFORMATION REPORTED BY WAVE

	Crime	Arrest	Trial	Post-conviction	Exoneration	All Waves
Name	98 (117)	96 (167)	98 (262)	90 (230)	73 (169)	91 (945)
Age	91 (108)	71 (123)	80 (213)	59 (150)	40 (91)	66 (685)
Job	55 (65)	35 (60)	29 (78)	38 (98)	24 (55)	34 (356)
Race	0 (0)	5 (8)	4 (12)	5 (13)	2 (15)	4 (38)

The cases involving teenage children and young adults also focused on their positive characteristics and the normative behaviors that were disrupted by violence. While there were only two cases involving victims who meet these age criteria, the data revealed a slight difference in how they were presented. The accounts of the deaths of these two victims had an underlying message of future promise. When a 17-year-old was missing in Omaha, Nebraska, she was not just a student, but a "dedicated, responsible and goal-oriented student" who was also "a member of the National Honor Society and the North High Student council" who was "looking forward to North's Oct. 2 homecoming, for which she is a queen candidate" (Burbach and Powell, 1992). Wave one accounts consistently referred to the young woman as a "homecoming queen candidate" and/or "honor student" who had not been seen since she "went to either mover her car or retrieve her book bag from the car" (Reilly and Powell, 1992). The other case, which involved an 18-year-old, presented her as a "boisterous," "funny," "community college student" (King and Stewart, 1986) who gave her "heart to Jesus" and was baptized (Vice, 1986). The tone and content of wave one accounts presented both victims as holding great promise to be upstanding members of their communities. Young children, however, were treated differently.

Children who are victimized by violent crime automatically invoke a sympathetic response from most readers. In these cases the young children who were killed were all victims of very violent deaths. The circumstances of the crimes and the ages of the child victims were sympathetic portraits by default, but the reports went beyond these factors. The cases involving children tended to present them as happy children who were doing normative, child-like things. For example, when a woman, her two daughters, and young niece were killed, wave one accounts made a point of reporting that two of the children were seen "playing in a small swimming pool" by a neighbor "less than an hour before" they were found dead "clad in their swimsuits" (Mckinnon, 1994). When another woman and two of her young daughters were found murdered, the paper reported that days before their deaths the five year old had "made her mom a little Mother's Day card" (Couch, 1985). Regardless of the victim's age, a majority of wave one accounts presented them as particularly sympathetic characters who were undeserving of the violence they encountered.

The victims continued to be the primary focus of articles in wave two. The articles provided basic demographic information on the victims, though to a lesser degree than in wave one. The victim's age was reported in 71% (n=123) of articles and the name was reported in 96.5% (n=167). Only 4.6% (n=8) reported the victim's race with 35% (n=60) reporting the victim's job. The articles continued to present the victims as sympathetic characters, with 61.3% (n=106) of articles containing these references. Only 1.2% (n=2) of wave two articles made negative references to the victims.

A majority of articles in wave two presented the victims as sympathetic characters. The patterns revealed in wave one continued, the victims were still presented as good people who had their normative, positive life experiences disrupted by violence. For example, after the arrest of Timothy Hennis, it was consistently reported that the victim had only met Hennis because her Air Force Captain husband was being transferred to England and the family could not take their dog. The victim placed an advertisement in the newspaper and Hennis adopted the pet (see Krisher and Jones, 1985). A wave two account reporting the arrest of Joseph Green described the victim as "very family-oriented" "fun loving" and "a real pleasure to work with." The accounts focused on the fact that the woman was working outside when confronted by an assailant (Greenberg, 1992).

The victims were no longer the main characters in wave three stories. The articles continued to provide basic demographic information, but the attempts to personalize the victims and present them as sympathetic characters declined. The victim's age was reported in 80% (n=213) of articles and the name was reported in 98% (n=262). Only 4.5% (n=12) reported the victim's race and 29% (n=78) reported the victim's job. Only 46% (n=124) of the articles presented the victims as sympathetic characters, and 7% (n=18) even reported on negative victim characteristics.

Wave three accounts contained one major change in how they presented the victims as sympathetic characters. While the references decreased in wave three, the themes also changed. They were still presented as good people whose lives were disrupted by violence, however, the focus shifted to how their deaths had impacted others. This theme was most likely to be present in articles reporting convictions and death verdicts. For example, when Warren Manning was convicted of murdering a South Carolina state trooper, the victim's wife was quoted as saying: "I feel like I don't have a life to go back to" (Hinshaw, 1989a). When Shareef Cousin received a death sentence, the victim's father said "my life is like a black void, a hole. I can't sleep at night" (Varney, 1996a). Sympathetic victim references usually involved a combination of these factors. The statement from the victim's friend or family member was often in the context of the victim as a good person. When a death verdict was returned for Ray Krone the victim's mother described the last time she saw her daughter. She reported that the victim had said "I love you, Mama." The mother told the court: "That has to last me for the rest of my life... It is not enough" (Kwok, 1992a). These statements indicated that the victim was a good, loving daughter. The presentations of sympathetic victims was a significant factor in the legitimation of the death penalty in these cases. More importantly, however, was the dichotomous presentation of good victims and evil defendants.

THE DEFENDANTS

Defendants were consistently presented as people who were guilty of committing heinous crimes. Twenty-five defendants made their first appearances in wave two accounts, and they quickly became a major focus of the articles. Basic demographic information was provided, though not to the same degree as for victims. The defendant's race was reported in only five wave two articles and only 27% (n=46) reported the defendant's job. The defendants were overwhelmingly presented as guilty of the crimes, with 65% (n=113) of wave two articles including statements that alluded to the defendant's guilt. Only 14% (n=24) of wave two articles indicated in any way that the defendant may not be guilty of the crime. In addition to being presented as guilty, the defendants were presented in a general negative way. Negative references were made to the defendant in 46% (n=80) of wave two accounts.

The defendants were the main characters in wave three reports. The attention they received, however, was primarily negative. Basic demographic information increased slightly from wave two. The defendant's race was reported in 3.7% (n=10) of articles and 35% (n=94) reported the defendant's job. Guilty representations increased over wave two, with 70% (n=187) of articles including statements that alluded to the defendant's guilt. One major difference in wave three accounts was that 38% (n=100) indicated in that the defendant may not be guilty of the crime. General negative references declined slightly, with only 39% (n=104) containing negative information about the defendant.

GUILTY DEFENDANTS

Wave two and three articles consistently included statements, or had an overt tone that indicated the defendant was guilty of the crime. This was primarily accomplished through descriptions of state's evidence. This is problematic in wave two because information only becomes evidence when entered into and accepted as such in court. The newspapers consistently presented the information as factual evidence and rarely questioned its credibility or validity. The presentation of the defendant as guilty of the crime peaked in wave three accounts. The articles focused heavily on the state's presentation of evidence, which often achieved a guilty theme. Reports also heavily quoted prosecutors' in court statements that were not flattering to the defendants. Wave two and three articles primarily relied on descriptions of eyewitness identifications, confessions, and physical evidence to present the defendants as guilty.

Eyewitness identifications were presented as proof of guilt without any questions of their veracity. They were usually cited as the reason an individual became a suspect. For example, it was reported that Frank Lee Smith was arrested "after being identified as the suspect by witnesses who saw him climb from the little girl's bedroom window" (Connelly, 1985b). In the next account of his arrest a police detective indicated that the composite drawing facilitated by the eyewitnesses "turned out to be so good that when we put it out on the streets, people immediately recognized it as a man from that area" (Connelly, 1985a). In another case, the paper reported that the "police arrested Cousin after two witnesses identified him in a photo lineup" (Philbin, 1995). Timothy Hennis was seen "getting into a white Chevrolet Chevette" in front of the victims' home. The eyewitness then picked his "picture out of a group of photographs" (Krisher, 1985b). In Joseph Green's case "several witness and Miscally [the victim] were able to give police a description of the suspect" One witness "later identified a man as the killer through a one-way mirror" (Greenberg, 1992). Wave three accounts gave even greater credence to eyewitness testimony. When Shareef Cousin's trial began the prosecutor was quoted as encouraging the jury to trust the eyewitness's "positive identification. When she turned around she saw Shareef cousin with a gun in (Gerardi's) face, and she saw him shoot (Gerardi) in the face" (Varney, 1996b). The next report described the testimony from the eyewitness. While pointing at Cousin, she said "I will never forget that face" (Varney, 1996c). Wave three accounts also rarely questioned the validity of eyewitness testimony. Instead, through the tone of the articles it was presented as proof of the defendant's guilt. The motives of the witness were never questioned in wave three accounts, they were presented as being certain and even doing the right thing. In the case of William Nieves, a "33-year-old prostitute" could "hold her head a little higher" after "she did her duty as a citizen" and testified that she saw Nieves kill a man over a drug debt (Racher, 1994).

Eyewitness testimony was further validated when it came from alleged accomplices. These cases consistently reported that the defendant was not only the perpetrator of the crime, but that the alleged accomplice had witnessed the victim's death. Despite the fact that the alleged accomplices always claimed to be less culpable than the defendants, wave three accounts never questioned the motives of these witnesses. Jeremy Sheets' case was replete with accounts of his alleged accomplice's confession. Despite the fact that the man killed himself before trial, the uncross-examined statement was played in court. It was quoted extensively in the trial reports, particularly the part in which the alleged accomplice described how Sheets allegedly killed and raped the victim. The alleged accomplice "just stood there and did nothing" while Sheets stabbed the victim "at least three or four times" and then "began raping" her (Brunkow, 1997a). One of Joseph Burrows' alleged accomplices testified that Burrows had beaten her before he "smiled as he shot the victim in the head" after ignoring her plea to spare the man's life (Rooney, 1989a). In addition to eyewitness testimony, the articles heavily reported alleged confessions when they were a factor.

In cases involving alleged defendant confessions, the articles mentioned them in every report. As with eyewitness testimony, the integrity of the confessions was never questioned. The articles that reported "confessions" contained two interesting similarities. First, it was overwhelmingly reported that the confessions were given to third parties, not investigating officers. For example, Joaquin Jose Martinez allegedly confessed to his wife while police listened "via a hidden microphone." The paper reported that "Martinez talked about his role in the murders.... he clearly implicated himself" (Shaver, 1996). Steve Manning reportedly "confessed to killing" the victim during conversations with his cellmate (Wilson, 1993).

Second, the confessions were not presented as contrite or remorseful, they were presented as boastful, arrogant accounts of the crimes, or how the defendant would get away with murder. For example, Thomas Kimbell reportedly "boasted" to a hitchhiker "about having committed the murders" He reportedly said that the easy part was "getting in and out." The information contained in the alleged confession, according to police, could not have been "known by anyone except the killer" (Mcdevitt, 1997). In another case, Gary Wayne Drinkard "bragged to his half sister and her common-law husband that he wouldn't be arrested." He also "laughed about the shooting" (Surratt, 1993). Alleged defendant confessions were consistently reported as proof of guilt. When they were not a factor in a case, reports of physical evidence tying the defendant to the crime played a more significant role.

The third major guilty theme involved the description of physical evidence. Again, wave two accounts failed to question the veracity of the evidence, or its scientific validity. It was always presented as proof that the police had arrested the culpable party. For example, "a major break came when Carl Lawson's fingerprints and footprints were discovered at the scene of the crime" (Sorkin, 1989). Robert Lee Miller was arrested "after police matched his blood type to samples found at the murder scenes" (Thornton, 1987c). Randall Padgett was arrested after "a DNA match between" his blood and "semen found at the crime scene" (Nichols, 1992a).

Wave three accounts also focused on descriptions of physical evidence as proof of guilt, and the validity of the evidence was rarely disputed in the articles. The key evidence in Randall Padgett's trial was a "DNA match" (Nichols, 1992d). For Ray Krone it was the "striking similarity in both pattern and shape" between his teeth and the bite-marks left on the victim (Kwok, 1992b). Accounts of Timothy Hennis' trial repeatedly included statements indicating that a piece of burned corduroy fabric found in a barrel in his back yard could have made the "bloody fabric impressions" found at the murder scene (Ruffin, 1986a). Carl Lawson left his "calling card - footprints from his tennis shoes in blood next to the body" (Bosworth, 1990). While undisputed descriptions of eyewitness accounts, physical evidence, and confessions were important to presenting the defendants as guilty and legitimating the death penalty, both were also achieved by presenting them as bad people.

BAD PEOPLE

The presentations of the defendants' character functioned to legitimize the death penalty. The defendants were presented as deserving the harshest punishment because they were bad people arrested for horrible crimes. The two most common types of presentations of the defendants as bad people were reports of general negative characteristics and prior criminal history. Negative characteristics involved a hodgepodge of issues. For example, two defendants were consistently described as members of street gangs, another was a former corrupt police officer. One was consistently described as a racist, while others were described as drug users, drug dealers, and alcoholics.

The primary issue involving the defendants' character was prior crimes. The defendants were presented as thugs, violent career offenders, anomalous killers, or crazy killers. Thugs were those who had been convicted of property crimes, drug offenses, other non-violent offenses, and minor violence. The articles tended to portray the homicide charges as being a natural progression for an individual who had a long criminal history. For example, when Carl Lawson was arrested, he was a "member of the Disciples street gang" who had been "convicted of aggravated battery for beating another girlfriend" (Sorkin, 1989). Thomas Kimbell not only "frequently beat" his former girlfriend and "abused her children," he also beat "his parents several times" (Smith, 1996). When Shareef Cousin, a juvenile, was arrested for murder during an armed robbery the paper pointed out: "it wasn't the first time Cousin has been arrested." The article then described his arrest for "carrying a concealed weapon" his time in drug rehabilitation, and even the "Cs and Ds" that "dominate his academic record" (Philbin and Baker, 1995).

Defendants with prior convictions or allegations of violence were presented as violent career offenders. The articles described prior crimes, convictions, and sentences. The message sent by these articles was not subtle. Under the headline "Paroled Killer Charged in Rape of Girl" Frank Lee Smith's criminal history was thoroughly detailed. He "has admitted to killing twice, beginning when he was 13 years old" (Connelly, 1985a). The article included descriptions of the crimes, and revealed that Smith "was sentenced to life in prison for first-degree murder. He served 15 years" (Connelly, 1985a). Joseph Green was described as having "a long criminal history. He has served three years for second-degree murder and 2 ½ years for battery of a correctional officer" (*Gainesville Sun*, 1993).

The presentation of defendants as violent career offenders did not stop at convictions, it also included suspicions. Five cases involved articles that attempted to tie the defendants to other unsolved crimes of violence. When Robert Hayes was arrested for the murder of a woman at a Florida horse track, the paper reported that "there are certain similarities" between the Florida homicide and what had been declared a suicide death at a New York track. Due to Hayes' arrest, New York police "reopened the case and are considering exhuming the body" (Roth, 1990). Steve Manning became "a suspect in several suburban Chicago killings" including "the killing of his father" (O'Brien, 1992). After police arrested Walter McMillian for the murder of Ronda Morrison, they also charged him with homicide in the death of another woman. This was despite the fact that "no connections have been made" between the two homicides (Lett, 1987).

Defendants who had no criminal histories were presented as anomalous killers. They were presented as guilty of the crimes, but the articles contained an underlying tone that indicated the crimes were out-of-character. These defendants, however, were still subject to negative representations. For example, Andrew Golden was described as "a former teacher" who was charged with drowning his "wife of 24 years." The accounts reported that "he had been fired" from his job for "lying about having a Ph.D." and he "told investigators he had no insurance" when he had "policies valued at $353,000" (Foushee, 1991a). Another account outlined his enormous debts and that he "lied about assets" when seeking loans (Foushee, 1991c). These accounts clearly indicate that the crime may have been out-of-character, but

Golden was a liar who was heavily in debt and killed his wife to collect insurance money. Gary Gauger was described as a "gentle farmer" who "picked insects off by hand." He also "struggled with a drinking problem" and had lost his driver's license "because of two drunken-driving convictions." According to police, he "finally came out and said he killed" his parents (McRoberts, 1993b). Again, this article sent the message that the crime may have been out-of-character for Gauger, but he was not a great person, lending credence to the notion that he was guilty as charged.

Timothy Hennis was also presented in this way. The day after his arrest, the *Fayetteville Observer Times* ran two articles side-by-side on the front page, under a large photo of a handcuffed Hennis being taken to jail. The first article appeared under the headline "Affidavit Puts Hennis At Death Site" and reports that "a man who was walking in front of the victims' home saw Hennis leaving the house." It described how Hennis met the victim, an Air Force captain's wife, and the "evidence" police had seized from his home (Krisher, 1985b). The second article appeared under the headline: "Arrest 'Surprises' Hennis' Neighbors" and reported that Hennis "seemed" to be a "heck of a nice guy" who has a "baby" of his own. According to his neighbors, "it just didn't seem like he'd do something like that." The article pointed out that Hennis was a parachute rigger in the Army, an enlisted man who "did not like being in the Army and was anxious to get out." The underlying tone that was present in this account is that Hennis was a recluse. He did not interact with his neighbors. One neighbor reported that "they never came out of the house except to do yard work" and the article reported "few... said they had talked with" Hennis (Jones, 1985). In a military community, the fact that an enlisted man was accused of killing the wife and two children of an Air Force captain was an important distinction. The fact that Hennis was a private man who did not often communicate with his neighbors indicated that he may have had a darker side.

Other defendants were presented as crazy killers. This representation was reserved for those who may or may not have had prior criminal histories, but whose behavior was impacted by mental illness. For example, Robert Lee Miller was presented as a crazy killer. He was arrested after telling the police that he had dreams about the separate murders of two elderly women. It was determined that he would "be sent to a mental hospital" for evaluation (*Daily Oklahoman*, 1987a) where it was determined that he could participate in his own defense (*Daily Oklahoman*, 1987b). The testimony at the preliminary hearing was described in one account and referred to in subsequent reports. The testimony revealed that during police questioning Miller complained of "demons, spirits and spells" and that the "two dead women had appeared to him in a dream and asked him to help police solve the crime." It was reported that Miller "described the killings in detail as he recalled his dreams" and that he "accurately" described "door locks and how glass on one back door was broken" (Clay, 1987). The reports of Miller's case clearly presented him as a mentally disturbed man who had committed two violent crimes. While these types of character assaults on the defendants were used in waves two and three, negative presentations assumed an additional technique in wave three.

Wave three accounts tended to present the defendants as guilty by reporting that they were not remorseful or showed no emotion. This theme, along with a focus on state's evidence resulted in a tone that suggested the defendant was guilty of the crime. When Larry Osborne was sentenced to death, he "showed no visible emotion... nor did he express any remorse for the killings" (White, 1999). Frank Lee Smith "shouted obscenities at the jury" when he was convicted (Springer, 1986a), but showed "no emotion" when the death verdict was read because he did not "think it would do any good" (Springer, 1986b).

The defendants were also presented as being defiant in light of their convictions or the strong cases against them. This was exemplified in the report of Warren Manning's death verdict. Prior to jury deliberations, Manning testified "if you give me life, maybe I'll have a chance to prove my innocence." The prosecutor said: "he insulted the jury... They knew it was him. It was him; there's no question about it" (Hinshaw, 1989b). During the prosecutor's closing arguments in Shareef Cousin's sentencing hearing, Shareef yelled "I wasn't out there either!" The prosecutor "triumphantly grabbed the moment" and said: "that's the face Michael Gerardi saw pointing a gun at him; that's the anger he saw" (Varney, 1996a). When Robert Lee Miller "denied he was the killer" and "ask for a special prayer for the jurors for they know not what they done" the prosecutor pointed out that Miller knew "details only the killer would know" (Clay, 1988).

Fifteen cases that involved wave three accounts included quotes from defendants who said they were not guilty. Jeremy Sheets said "I've never killed anybody" (Brunkow, 1997b). Walter McMillian said "I didn't kill that girl" (Shaw, 1988). Alfred Rivera told the victims' mothers "I ain't killed your son" (Bauerlein, 1997) and Timothy Hennis said "I'm not guilty" (Ruffin, 1986c). Steve Manning told the court he was "an innocent man" (O'Brien, 1993). Joseph Burrows told the court that his accuser and alleged accomplice "used her own gun and laid the blame on me" (Rooney, 1989b). She eventually recanted and admitted that she had acted alone in the murder, but implicated Burrows to avoid a death sentence. Ray Krone warned the court "the real killer is still walking out there" (Kwok, 1992a). Years later, DNA validated his statement. At the time the statements were made, they were presented as being made by defiant killers who refused to admit their guilt.

The defendants were presented by wave two and three accounts as bad people who were guilty of committing very heinous crimes. Regardless of their life situations prior to the charges the newspapers consistently found ways to present them in a negative way. If they had prior convictions they were thugs or violent career offenders. If they had no prior convictions there was something about them that was different. In short, the defendants were presented as different from the rest of society. Presenting them as evil, mean, or just different successfully worked to legitimize the punishment to be meted out. An additional technique also functioned to support the notion the death penalty as appropriate. It involved the way the police were presented.

THE POLICE

The actions of the police received much attention in wave one accounts. While this attention waned in subsequent waves, it laid an important foundation. In wave one, the police were the primary source of information, but their activities were also heavily reported. Wave one reports consistently presented the police as crime solvers. In fact, 67% (n=80) of wave one accounts presented the police in this way. This was primarily accomplished through an underlying tone that indicated the police would solve the crime. When an arrest was not immediate and there were wave one accounts, the articles focused on the frustration of the police rather than their inability to solve the crime.

This tone of expectation resulted in a portrait of the police as crime solvers. In Robert Miller's case, five months lapsed between the first homicide and his arrest. The police department formed a task force of "nine detectives and three supervisors," but still found it "frustrating." One officer said "it just takes time. You've just got to keep plugging away at leads" (Thornton, 1987a). Despite the lack of an arrest or even a strong suspect after five months of investigation, the tone of the articles was supportive of police efforts and even sent the message to the reader that the police would solve the crime. This message was also apparent in wave one accounts in Jeremy Sheets' case, despite the fact that four years lapsed between the crime and Sheets' arrest. The articles focused on what the police were doing rather than what they had not done. For example, almost two years after the victim disappeared the paper reported: "The case has frustrated homicide detectives... and it remains a priority. They have interviewed hundreds of people and have searched at least two vehicles" (Powell, 1994).

The crime solver theme was often achieved through a report of the addition of multiple agencies or investigators, special equipment, and the use of jargon. For example, one reported that "two members of the city's mobile crime unit" were performing the investigation due to their "expertise in evaluating crime-scene evidence" (Mckinnon, 1994). Another reported that "The police homicide unit has devoted... six full-time officers to the case" (Anderson, 1992). Often, a combination of these factors was present. For example, during the investigation of the Hennis case the following was reported:

> State Bureau of Investigation evidence technicians and sheriff's detectives entered the home... about 7 p.m. Monday. Some didn't leave until 1:30 a.m.... A source said the investigators were using a lumination system that helps spot blood stains. (Krisher, 1985b).

In other cases, it was not so subtle. When Ronda Morrison was found murdered in Alabama, the local sheriff was quoted as saying:

> Although we cannot release to the public information on leads we are following because it could jeopardize our investigation, we want local citizens to know that we have many law-

enforcement officials working night and day to solve this case. (Stewart and Lett, 1986).

This statement by the sheriff appeared beside a photograph of an "investigator" taking fingerprints at the scene. While the content of what was reported was most important to the crime solver image, the language used certainly solidified the message. In some accounts police were "seeking clues" (*Tulsa World*, 1985). In others they "extended their crime-scene tape" (Goldberg, 1996). Some "canvassed the neighborhood" (Thornton and Ellis, 1986), while others "asked the public to be on the lookout" (*Farmerville Gazette*, 1986). Regardless of the circumstances, geographic area, or newspaper size, the use of police jargon was common and successfully invoked an image of the police as crime solvers.

The significance of the police as crime solvers is twofold. First, presenting the police in this way reinforced the dominant social control ideology. It is a reminder to the public that the police are the enforcers of the state's power. Using the police as the primary sources of information worked to impart their crime control message on the public. The police agenda was clearly and consistently presented. This included presenting police agencies and their duties in a positive light. Presenting them in this way reinforces the dominant ideology by suppressing questions of their tactics or agenda. Second, presenting the police as crime solvers reinforced the notion that the culpable party had been arrested. This functioned to discourage doubts about a defendants' guilt. While the presentation of the police as crime solvers was significant, it was the interaction of the various factors that worked to legitimize the death penalty in these cases.

OVERVIEW

The reports in waves one, two, and three appeared prior to the canonical events. They were prompted by the discovery of the crimes, investigative developments, arrests, pre-trial hearings, jury selection, trial testimony, and verdicts, among others. The patterns of themes in these articles legitimized capital punishment as public policy by presenting information that was supportive of the death penalty for a defendant charged with a particular crime. This was accomplished by presenting the crimes as heinous and as public problems, the victims as sympathetic, and the defendants as bad people who were guilty of the charges. The articles further legitimized the death penalty in these cases by presenting the police as crime solvers. This factor functioned to alleviate potential doubt about the defendants' guilt, which assisted in presenting the death penalty as appropriate. Individually, each of these components reinforced the state's agenda. As a combination, however, they were a powerful legitimating force.

CHAPTER 6

Delegitimizing the Death Penalty

Post-conviction and exoneration reports delegitimized both the individual convictions and the death penalty. Wave four articles were prompted by a variety of issues, including appeals, reversals, the discovery of new evidence, changes in the state's case, and pre-retrial hearings. These accounts marked the beginning of the canonical events. In most cases the issues that led to the exonerations first arose in wave four accounts. Wave five accounts began with the release of a defendant, jury or bench trial acquittals, or the dropping of charges. The articles in wave five were prompted by these issues as well as by defendants' lawsuits and debates over modifications in capital punishment statutes. Wave five also contained examinations of the cases to determine how the wrongful conviction occurred, the defendant's life after death row, and even "infamous" crimes. In short, the articles in these waves were diverse and assumed an individual character.

Reports of canonical events, or script disruptions in waves four and five were descriptions of issues that automatically worked to delegitimize the death penalty. These reports of system mistakes acknowledged the fallibility of the system. They reported that an innocent person could have been executed. Reports that raised questions about the state's cases, presented the defendants as not guilty, or clearly indicated that a mistake had been made functioned to delegitimize the death penalty. The articles also, however, worked to relegitimize capital punishment. The issues that led to the wrongful convictions and ultimate exonerations were diverse (see Appendix A). What is important, however, is that despite the dissimilarity of the actual errors, the reports of those errors still contained common themes that worked to relegitimize the death penalty.

Wave four accounts raised serious questions about the integrity of the states' cases. These questions were usually raised unwittingly. They were rarely the result of in-depth investigations by reporters. Rather, they were merely reports of issues raised on appeal. These issues, whether they were argued before review courts, cited as reasons for reversal, or just cited as changes in the states cases, automatically functioned to delegitimize capital punishment. They are clear indicators of the potential for error in the system. The notion that the system functions to punish only the guilty is vital to the legitimacy of capital punishment. The articles in wave four did function to delegitimize the convictions and the death penalty, but they also simultaneously began the process of relegitimation. This process was continued in wave five.

WAVE FOUR

Wave four marked the onset of the canonical events in 27 cases. Only two cases were without wave four articles. Coverage in nine cases began with reports of serious questions about the integrity of the states' cases and the defendants' guilt. Articles in the remaining 18 cases began by describing the appeals process during which perfunctory issues were raised, but progressed into reports of issues that delegitimized the convictions. Two significant issues were revealed from wave four accounts. First, they functioned to delegitimize the convictions. This was accomplished by reporting information that cast doubt on the defendant's guilt. The information reported to this end included descriptions of new evidence, changes in the states' cases, and flawed investigations. Significantly, however, these articles also contained relegitimizing information. Second, the articles that continued to present the defendant as guilty functioned to legitimize the death penalty as public policy by focusing on appeals as perfunctory protections provided to guilty defendants.

DELEGITIMIZING AND RELEGITIMIZING THE CONVICTIONS

A multitude of issues that would lead to the canonical events emerged in wave four accounts. As a result, the tone and content of the articles underwent significant change. For the first time in the metastories, 54%

(n=137) included information that indicated that the defendants could be factually innocent of the crimes. This was accomplished through a focus on new evidence or problems with the states' cases. The significance of these delegitimizing factors is that they appeared alongside issues that functioned to relegitimize the conviction.

New evidence primarily involved advances in DNA testing, previously unknown witnesses, and reinterpretations of old evidence. Each of these issues was presented as casting doubt on the integrity of the convictions, but they were presented in a way that relegitimized them. Relegitimation was achieved in three ways. First the articles described strong cases against the defendants. Second, they suggested that the information could not have been known at the time of the trial. Third, they presented sarcastic comments from system functionaries that attempted to delegitimize the idea that a mistake had been made.

The first technique involved a description of the new evidence followed by a review of the original evidence. This was exemplified when the *Chicago Tribune* reported that Cook County state's attorney's office asked the Illinois Supreme Court to vacate Ronald Jones' conviction. The article reported that "DNA tests... concluded that semen recovered from the body" of the victim "could not have come from Jones" (Martin, 1997). After discussing the role DNA played in other exonerations, the article described the "evidence" against Jones. It stated that Jones had been a suspect in a previous rape that was "similar enough" to the crime in question. A witness also told police that Jones had "tried to panhandle" the victim "hours before the murder" (Martin, 1997). Most importantly, however, "Jones confessed to killing" the victim (Martin, 1997). This article clearly delegitimized the original conviction and death sentence by reporting the DNA excluded Jones as the depositor of the semen. It relegitimized the conviction by describing the circumstantial evidence and Jones' confession.

This pattern was consistent in wave four accounts involving new evidence. Three years after Ray Krone was sentenced to death, a pending appeal prompted the *Phoenix Gazette* to report that his attorney had "piled up evidence that indicates" he "may not have killed" the victim. That new evidence included "DNA testing that exonerates Krone" (Dodd, 1995). After describing the pile of new evidence, the article explained that the victim was reportedly meeting "Ray" after work, his bite marks were "consistent with the mark on" the victim's breast, that "small plastic beads" were found with the body and in Krone's car, and that he had "no solid alibi" (Dodd, 1995). It is important to note that Ray Krone was granted a new trial, though not based on new evidence. Only three of the eight post-conviction/pre-trial reports that followed the report described above even mentioned the new DNA tests. Instead, they focused on the bite marks that "linked" (Manson, 1995) Krone to the murder in the "prosecution's slam-dunk case" (Leonard, 1995a; see also Brown , 1995; Leonard, 1995b). Krone was convicted a second time based on bite mark testimony.

In addition to focusing on the evidence of guilt, the articles also relegitimized the convictions and the death penalty by indicating the information could not have been known at the time of the original trial. This technique was predominately used when evolutions in science led to the discovery of "new evidence," primarily DNA. For example, when the Florida Supreme Court ordered a retrial for Robert Hayes because of "scientifically shaky" DNA tests used during the first trial, the *Sun Sentinel* lauded the court for affirming "the overall value of DNA evidence" (Hirth and Jensen, 1995). The article reported that DNA testing revealed that a "hair found clutched in the victim's hand suggested the crime might have been committed by a white man" (Hirth and Jensen, 1995). Hayes is African-American. The report included a description of the evidence against Hayes including "DNA evidence" that "linked him to the crime." It further indicated that DNA testing "is still evolving and must be evaluated on a case-by-case basis." The fact that Hayes is black and DNA indicated a white man likely committed the murder was almost lost in the article. It described the old "band shifting" DNA test and suggested that the error was due to the use of the now "debunked" method (Hirth and Jensen, 1995). This technique did not always require such lengthy diatribes, usually it was handled with a simple statement: "DNA testing at the time was not sophisticated enough to provide reliable results" (Martin, 1997). Similarly, during Ray Krone's second post-conviction phase it was "the *latest* DNA technology" that finally prompted the state to recognize that a mistake had been made (emphasis added; DeFalco, 2002a).

The third relegitimation technique used in light of new evidence involved direct attempts by system functionaries to delegitimize the new evidence. This form of "problem denial" is consistent with the research of Benford and Hunt (2003). For example, in Ray Krone's first post-conviction phase, in the same report that described the "DNA testing that exonerates" him, the prosecutor was quoted as saying "Everybody in prison's innocent. Just ask them" (Dodd, 1995). In another case involving bite mark evidence, Greg Wilhoit sought a new trial based on the fact that his defense attorney had failed to call experts to rebut the state's forensic odontologist. When the president of the American Board of Forensic Odontology, Dr. Thomas Krauss, and 10 others unanimously agreed that "the bite mark found on the body" of the victim "was not made by" Wilhoit, the prosecutor shrugged it off. He said "As far as Dr. Krauss goes, that doesn't bother me because he is getting paid to say those things" (East, 1990a). He went on to say that Wilhoit "had no alibi."

The prosecutor in Robert Miller's case consistently attempted to delegitimize the new evidence and relegitimize Miller's conviction and death sentence. During Miller's first trial prosecutors contended that "it was Miller's semen" found at both crime scenes. After seven years on death row, DNA tests which were "not routinely done in Oklahoma County in 1987" revealed that "it was not Miller's semen found" at the crime scenes (Godfrey, 1995). The DNA had not only exonerated Miller, but had indicated that the crimes were likely committed by a man who was convicted of two other rapes in the same neighborhood. These facts did not convince the prosecutor of Miller's innocence. He said the tests only "prove that Miller didn't act alone" and that the evidence that convicted Miller was "still valid" (Godfrey, 1995). The same prosecutor continued these messages in subsequent reports.

Not all cases involved new physical evidence. The questionability of Joseph Burrows' guilt was prompted by the discovery of a new alibi witness. Burrows had always maintained that he was at his brother's home watching television at the time of the murder. The state did not believe his alibi witnesses, nor did the jury. During Burrows' third year on death row a woman who was with him the night of the murder spoke out. She had moved to Arizona and did not return to Illinois to testify at his trials. Defense attorneys located her and she spoke to the *Champaign-Urbana News Gazette*. She revealed that not only was she with Burrows the night of the murder, but that the female co-defendant who had implicated Burrows, had confessed to her the day after the murder (Rooney, 1991). Faced with this new information, the prosecutor said "We blew holes in (Burrows') alibi.... I don't see any change in the story" (Rooney, 1991). Other cases, however, did not involve the discovery of new evidence. Instead, the canonical events were prompted by problems with the states' cases.

The three primary problems that plagued the state's cases were witness issues, prosecutorial misconduct, and evidence reliability. In light of these issues, the convictions were relegitimized through descriptions of other evidence, attacks on witnesses, descriptions of strong cases, and denials of problems. Witness problems involved recantations, competency, and perjury. Recantations of codefendants were a major factor in wave four accounts. For example, three years after Ralph Myers testified that Walter McMillian had killed the victim, he changed his story. He reportedly told the court that his "drug counseling and therapy program" prompted him to develop "the courage to try to do something about my role in putting an innocent man on death row" (Handley, 1991). Myers also indicated that he had been pressured by police and prosecutors to implicate McMillian and that he was "shown pictures of the crime scene that helped [him] make up the testimony" (Handley, 1991). After a series of hearings about the recantation the judge denied McMillian's appeal for a retrial (Handley, 1992a). In denying the motion, the judge ruled that none of the information provides "conclusive evidence that [Myers] perjured himself at the original trial." Instead, the judge found that the "pressure has been brought to bear" by defense attorneys for McMillian.

In essence, the judge ignored Myers' recantation and concluded that McMillian's defense attorneys had pressured him to alter his story. While the judge ignored the recantation, *60 Minutes* did not. In November 1992, *60 Minutes* aired an expose of the case (Handley, 1992b; *The Monroe Journal*, 1992; Handley, 1992c). It raised serious questions about McMillian's guilt and supported Myers' recantation. Two months after the episode, the paper ran an article about the case under the headline "Morrison Case Was Never Closed" (*Monroe Journal*, 1993a). Three months after the expose, it reported that the state was "taking a fresh look at the murder" (Stewart, 1993a), one week later the judge ordered a new trial for Walter McMillian (see Handley, 1993a). Despite the reports' delegitimation of McMillian's conviction, these accounts also contained relegitimation efforts.

The relegitimation effort most commonly used in reports of the witness recantation involved attempts to discredit the recantation. In

McMillian's case, the accounts focused on the fact that defense attorneys had met with the witness "12 to 15 times" and that they had told him they were the his attorneys (Handley, 1992d). The paper focused heavily on this issue as a means of not only delegitimizing the recantation, but relegitimizing McMillian's conviction. The reports attempted to cast doubt on the new statements. Additionally, the paper also reported that the recantation was prompted by the hiring of a hit man. The prosecutor was quoted as saying that a contract had been placed on the witness. He said the contract was "allegedly for Walter McMillian or on his behalf" and that the recantation came only after the witness "was told of the contract on his life" (Handley, 1992d). McMillian's case also involved allegations of prosecutorial misconduct.

Reports of prosecutorial misconduct before and during defendants' trials also worked to delegitimize the convictions and death penalty. In Joseph Burrows' case both of his alleged accomplices recanted their implications of Burrows. The female codefendant, who, it would later be learned, had committed the crime alone, alleged that the prosecutor "fed her information" and that she "spent hours coaching" the other alleged accomplice (Rooney, 1994a). The investigation by defense attorneys revealed that the two were in adjacent jail cells during Burrows' trial and that the prosecutor had met with both alleged accomplices together seven times (Rooney, 1994a). The obvious implication of this information is that the prosecutor coached the witnesses to improve their testimony and to reduce inconsistencies in their stories. In Walter McMillian's case it was alleged that during the trial, prosecutors failed to reveal plea arrangements made with witnesses (Shaw, 1991). In reversing Shareef Cousin's conviction, the Louisiana Supreme Court "criticized prosecutors" and ruled that "obviously exculpatory" statements by an eyewitness "should have been shared with defense attorneys" (Coyle, 1998). Defense attorneys also claimed that the prosecutor had hidden defense alibi witnesses. While the Louisiana Supreme Court did not rule on that issue, it was widely reported in subsequent reports.

Articles that reported allegations of prosecutorial misconduct also included relegitimation techniques. Primarily this involved denials (Benford and Hunt, 2003) or flippant comments by prosecutors that attempted to diminish the significance of the issue. For example when the Louisiana Supreme Court reversed Shareef Cousin's conviction and said the prosecutors engaged in "flagrant misuse of evidence" the prosecutor was quoted as saying he just "got carried away" in closing arguments (Coyle, 1998). He also said "I guess... a defendant with four armed robbery convictions tends to inflame us somewhat" (Coyle, 1998). Prosecutors in other cases consistently denied that they had withheld information from the defense (Shaw, 1991; Rooney, 1994a).

Evidentiary problems also plagued the states' cases and functioned to delegitimize the convictions. This category involved questions about the integrity of specific types of evidence used to convict a defendant. In wave four accounts these questions were reserved for bite mark evidence, jailhouse snitches, and uncross-examined witness accounts. Greg Wilhoit and Ray Krone were both convicted based on bite mark evidence. In Wilhoit's case the integrity of this type of evidence was not questioned. The articles merely focused on the fact that other experts concluded that Wilhoit's "teeth are drastically and dramatically different from the marks" on the victim, thereby "eliminating him as the perpetrator" (East, 1990b). In Krone's case, the integrity of bite marks as evidence came under serious scrutiny, but only during his second post-conviction phase. When new DNA tests exonerated him and indicated a known rapist had committed the murder the paper reported: "tooth mark identification is most effective when used in conjunction with other evidence, not as a sole determining factor for identity" (DeFalco, 2002b).

Steve Manning was convicted on "little more" than the testimony of a jailhouse informant (Mills and Armstrong, 1999a). When the case against him began to fall apart, the *Chicago Tribune* investigated the role of "snitches" in capital cases. The report criticized the state for allowing the testimony of a man who "lies about almost everything, even his own name." The article described the testimony and allowed the prosecutor to defend his use of a known liar. He indicated that the informant provided "information from Manning that only the killer would have known" and that he "didn't have any problem with his credibility" even though the snitch "is a scam artist" (Mills and Armstrong, 1999a).

The other evidentiary problem to arise in wave four accounts involved the use of uncross-examined witness statements. This issue was raised in two cases. Both Larry Osborne, in Kentucky, and Jeremy

Sheets, in Nebraska, were convicted on the statements of witnesses who had died before their trials. Both witnesses had provided statements to police prior to their deaths. The judges in both cases allowed the statements to be read to or played for the juries. The seriousness of the issue was not lost on the newspapers involved. They each indicated that it was a violation of a fundamental constitutional right. During Larry Osborne's post-conviction efforts the *Herald Leader* reported that "probably the most important right that a defendant has in a death penalty case is the ... right to confront your accusers" (*Herald Leader*, 2000). During Jeremy Sheets' post-conviction appeals the *Omaha World Herald* quoted a law professor who said: "The bottom line is, you have a fundamental right to confront your accuser. It's one of the basic tenets upon which this democracy was built" (Cooper, 1998). These accounts, however, also contained attempts to relegitimize the convictions.

In post-conviction reports in Jeremy Sheets' case, the descriptions of the "fundamental right to confront your accuser" were followed by a detailed analysis of exceptions to hearsay rules. The articles consistently described the "dying declarations" and "five common exceptions allowing hearsay" at trial (Cooper, 1998; Brunkow, 1999a; Brunkow, 1999b). In reports of Larry Osborne's appeals, the regional daily paper mentioned that "the law permits some exceptions to the rule" (*Herald Leader*, 2000). Other relegitimation technique were also present in these cases.

In the Sheets case, the articles provided information that supported the statements of the dead witness, thereby presenting the statements as accurate and Sheets as guilty. For example, Barnett, the dead witness, told police "Sheets raped her and stabbed her with a knife" (Tysver, 2000). To substantiate this claim, the article reported that the victim had "suffered three to four stab wounds... and had been sexually assaulted." Other articles reported that Barnett told police the crime was racially motivated and substantiated this by reporting that his statement was "filled with racial epithets" (Tysver, 1998). The weekly paper in the Osborne case used an additional technique. It consistently informed the reader that defense attorneys "were allowed to introduce *extensive testimony* about the various other contradictory statements" made by the dead witness (White, 2001 –emphasis added). Thus leaving the reader with the impression that the jury knew that the statements contained inconsistencies but still believed in Osborne's guilt.

In sum, the appearance of the issues that would lead to the canonical events worked to delegitimize the convictions, which functioned to delegitimize the death penalty in general. The appearance of new evidence and various problems with the states' cases presented a potential legitimacy crisis for these death penalty systems. Few wave four accounts, however, examined the death penalty as policy, or attempted to determine if the problems in a particular case were present in other cases. Instead, the articles used an individualistic approach and examined the issues in a single case. In doing so, the articles relegitimized the death penalty and the convictions by presenting the issues as problems with a particular case and by minimizing the error. These efforts, however, were not necessary in some accounts.

LEGITIMIZING DUE PROCESS

The remaining wave four accounts did not function to delegitimize the convictions. In 46% (n=118) of wave four reports the canonical events had not yet surfaced. These articles focused on developments in alleged accomplices' cases, lost appeals, collective death row inmate status, and victims' families. They continued to present the defendants as guilty, but they legitimized the death penalty differently. The articles that focused on alleged accomplices' cases simply mentioned that the defendant had already been convicted and was housed on death row. They reported that the alleged accomplices had testified against the defendant. For example, when the last of Joseph Burrows alleged accomplices was convicted the paper reported that she "cooperated with" the state and would received "a lot of consideration" (Rooney, 1989a). She "testified that Burrows ... shot the elderly man in the head..." Burrows "was convicted of being the triggerman and sentenced to death" (Rooney, 1989a).

The message sent by these reports was one of accuracy. The alleged accomplice actually witnessed the victim's death, and was so conscientious that they did the right thing and testified against the killer. When Alfred Rivera was on death row, "prosecutors tied up one last loose end" by allowing Rivera's alleged accomplice to plead guilty to lesser charges. The deal was "in exchange for testifying against... the triggerman [Rivera]" who "was convicted of first-degree murder... and sentenced to death" (Quinn, 1998). Essentially, these reports indicated that the most culpable party was convicted and on death row.

The articles that focused on filed or lost appeals presented them as perfunctory due process protections offered to guilty defendants. The issues argued before review courts were complicated issues, but the articles tended summarize them in a few words. These articles were short and contained very little information. They functioned to legitimize the death penalty by reporting on the appeals process in a way that indicated the issues raised were non-issues. For example, when Albert Burrell lost an appeal to the U.S. Supreme Court, the paper reported that the Court "let stand rulings that Burrell received a fair trial and properly was sentenced to death." Following a very brief description of the crime the article summarized the appeal:

> Burrell's appeal argued, among other things, that Louisiana's death penalty law is unconstitutional because anyone who pleads guilty to a capital murder charge avoids all possibility of the death penalty (*The Advocate*, 1991).

Unfortunately, the ruling was not published and therefore cannot be analyzed. The facts of the case, however, indicate that it is highly unlikely that this was the central focus of Burrell's appeal to the United States Supreme Court. The case involved a jailhouse informant. It was plagued by prosecutorial misconduct, witness perjury, and witness recantations. It is very likely that more substantial procedural issues were raised before the Supreme Court. The report, however, presented an issue that indicated that Burrell was guilty, and was not remorseful enough to confess to his crime.

In other cases, the reports of denied appeals reinforced the integrity of the original trials and convictions. A report of an appeal lost by Gary Drinkard revealed that he "contended there were numerous problems with jury selection" but the "appeals court turned back" the claims (*Decatur Daily*, 1998). Sporadic reports of appeals are, quite simply, reminders that the capital punishment system is legitimate because it contains safety mechanisms to protect against wrongful convictions, and to assure fairness in the process.

Other wave four accounts reported on the collective status of death row inmates. These reports literally listed each person housed on death row and contained a brief description of their alleged crimes. These accounts tended to focus on the appropriateness of capital punishment for the inmates and the fact that the wheels of justice turn slowly. For example, the "status" report present in Frank Lee Smith's case, reported that "Smith started killing at 13" and then describes two other homicides attributed to him. The article appeared under the headline "On Death Row, Prisoners Stall." A photo caption reveals that two inmates have been on death row "for more than 15 years" (Bulfin, 1990).

Articles of this type functioned to legitimize the death penalty by indicating that the appeals process was long and that death row inmates had ample access to due process. Time lines and dates were important components of these reports. For example, the "status" report published by *The State* categorized inmates by their appeal stages, including five who were "in the final appeals stage" (Butler, 1991). The report reminded readers that Warren Manning's case began when the crime occurred in 1988, Manning was sentenced in 1989, and "his appeal is being considered by the state Supreme Court" (Butler, 1991). Numerous other inmates included in the report had been on death row since the early 1980s. In addition to reminding their audience that death row inmates have ample access to due process, the articles legitimized their convictions by presenting them all as guilty of their crimes. For example, Steven Smith "fatally shot" the victim (Sherlock, 1990). Frank Lee Smith "raped and choked the child, then beat her to death with a rock" (Bulfin, 1990). Other wave four accounts, however, took a different approach.

Other post-conviction accounts focused on the families of victims. These articles provided very brief summaries of the events, the crimes were barely mentioned, and often the defendants' names were not included. These reports legitimized the death penalty by indicating the victims' families would receive some solace from the defendant's execution. For example, in a report of support among murder victims' families for a pending execution in South Carolina, the victim's wife in Warren Manning's case said "I hope I don't have to wait 11 years before justice is served" (Lore, Allard and Decker, 1990). In Greg Wilhoit's case, the victim's father said "I would pull the switch myself on this guy" (*Daily Oklahoman*, 1992). An article that mentioned

Shareef Cousin's case described the victim's family's "still-unsatisfied yearning for justice" (Varney, 1999). The assortment of articles from wave four that were sometimes only tangentially related to the cases functioned to legitimize the death penalty. They did so by presenting the defendants as guilty, the appeals process as lengthy, and the victims' families' satisfaction with the pending punishment. They failed to report any alternative explanations of the circumstances surrounding the victims' deaths, and presented the legal issues as perfunctory attempts by the defendants to avoid the inevitable. These issues, however, were a minority of wave four accounts. A majority of wave four accounts functioned to delegitimize the convictions. A majority also, however, contained efforts to relegitimize the convictions. The articles that appeared prior to changes in the cases functioned to legitimize the death penalty by reinforcing the notion that the system is fair and accurate. The cases changed drastically between waves four and five. As a result, the legitimation efforts also changed.

WAVE FIVE

The legitimacy crisis that was hinted at in wave four accounts came to fruition in wave five. The defendants in these cases had been convicted in 58% (n=611) of all the articles across all waves. Only 21% (n=222) of all articles indicated the system had failed the defendant with the conviction. The notion that the defendant may have been wrongfully convicted appeared in 30% (n=75) of wave four articles, but increased to 62% (n=143) in wave five accounts. The primary focus of wave five accounts was "how did this happen?" Importantly, the question involved a dichotomy. The articles not only asked how an innocent person ended up on death row, but they asked how a guilty person was freed. Regional daily papers were the most active in pursuing wave five issues. They were responsible for 71% (n=165) of exoneration articles. Local dailies and weeklies largely ignored these issues.

Wave five accounts had two primary themes, delegitimizing the exonerations and relegitimizing the death penalty as public policy. Only 13% (n=31) of wave five accounts had an overall tone that indicated the defendant was guilty. However, 90% (n=209) included statements that seriously questioned the defendants' guilt. The articles presented the exonerations as legal technicalities that freed guilty defendants or as legitimate responses to the circumstances.

DELEGITIMIZING THE EXONERATIONS

A majority of the exoneration reports presented them as legitimate responses to the various situations. In fact, 72% (n=168) of wave five accounts presented the exonerations in this way, while 18% (n=41) presented them as legal technicalities that freed guilty defendants. The remaining 10% (n=22) mentioned the exonerations in other contexts and provided so little information that themes were not discernible. The articles that presented the exonerations as technicalities focused on limits to the states' ability to retry the defendants. They described the evidence against the defendant and blamed review courts for limiting the options available to the state. In essence, when a defendant was presented as guilty, but given a second chance by review courts the reports sent the message that the problems were "legal technicalities." Often, this was a correct interpretation of the events. It was not new evidence or witness recantations that led to the reversals and exonerations, it was procedural error at the trial court level. In light of various errors, review courts excluded evidence, which placed limits on the state's ability to retry a defendant. When this occurred, the excluded evidence became a significant part of subsequent reports.

As previously discussed, both Jeremy Sheets and Larry Osborne were convicted on the uncross-examined testimony of dead witnesses. Their convictions and death sentences were reversed and remanded for retrials. In both cases the articles continued to present them as guilty, despite the fact that no physical evidence tied either of the defendants to the crimes. The prosecutors in both cases were precluded from using the statements of the dead witnesses. In turn, the prohibited evidence became the focus of subsequent articles. The articles consistently reminded readers that a legal technicality had led to an injustice. Osborne was retried on scant evidence and acquitted. Prosecutors in the Sheets case dropped the charges. The reports in these cases consistently reminded readers of the excluded evidence. In the Sheets case the *Omaha World Herald* reported:

> Prosecutors dropped the charges... after the Nebraska Supreme
> Court ruled they couldn't use a taped confession made by

Sheets' former roommate... who said the pair raped and killed Bush because she was black (Bleed, 2001).

The weekly paper in the Osborne case reminded readers that it was "initially a strong case" and that the Kentucky Supreme Court had excluded the testimony of the dead witness (White, 2002). In addition to these summaries in the body of the text, the articles that delegitimized the exonerations also contained statements from prosecutors that functioned similarly. For example, when Joseph Green was acquitted the paper described the statements of eyewitnesses, Green's criminal history, the original death verdict, and the reason the case was retried. The prosecutor was quoted as saying: "Anyone who says an innocent man has been vindicated is wrong. A guilty man has been set free because the courts have suppressed all the evidence" (Hutchens and Fischer, 2000).

In Randall Padgett's case, the prosecutor said that the acquittal does not mean Padgett is innocent, "only that the jury did not feel there was enough evidence to convict" (Nichols, 1997). When Robert Hayes was acquitted by a jury the prosecutor said that the excluded DNA evidence "probably had something to do with" the acquittal (Fitzgerald, 1997). When Larry Osborne was acquitted, the prosecutor spoke of the frustration of "knowing actually what happened but not being able to present testimony on it" (White, 2002). The case against Clarence Dexter ended because prosecutors literally lost evidence from the first trial. The prosecutor indicated that he had no choice but to drop the charges, "If I go forward... and lose and three weeks later they find these items, I'm going to look bad" (Williams, 1999).

When appellate courts ordered defendants released, the exonerations were delegitimized by summarizing the court rulings in a way that presented the defendant as guilty. While only two cases involved defendants who were ordered released by review courts, the articles assumed a particular tone. For example, when the Florida Supreme Court ordered the release of Andrew Golden because the state did not prove that his wife had been murdered, the paper described the case against him and quoted the court ruling as saying: "The finger of suspicion points heavily at Golden. A reasonable juror could conclude that he more likely than not caused his wife's death" (Foushee, 1994). Additionally, when the Illinois Supreme Court vacated Steven Smith's guilty verdict and death sentence, the *Chicago Tribune* reported that the court ruling "does not amount to a finding that Smith is innocent– only that the state had failed to prove him guilty" (Armstrong and Lighty, 1999).

It is important to reiterate that a large majority of exoneration articles presented the releases as rational ends to these cases. It was not, however, true in all cases. The cases that continued to present the defendants as guilty had a significant commonality. They all involved excluded evidence that limited the state's ability to retry the defendants. In these cases there was no smoking gun, DNA, or any other hard physical evidence that someone else was responsible for the crime. In sum, reasonable doubt existed regarding the defendants' innocence and the newspapers that reported on the cases chose to focus on the likelihood that they were, in fact, guilty. The articles that presented the exonerations as legitimate responses chose a different approach.

LEGITIMIZING THE EXONERATIONS

The releases, dropping of charges, and acquittals were presented as legitimate responses to the circumstances by 72% (n=168) of wave five accounts. This was accomplished mostly by an overall tone that indicated the defendant was innocent of the charges. The techniques that achieved that tone included describing evidence of innocence, an acceptance of the error by system functionaries, and the establishment of another suspect. Importantly, many of these techniques appeared in the same articles. Their combined effect was most important, but they also functioned individually to legitimize the exonerations.

The first technique involved descriptions of evidence that supported the notion that the defendants were innocent. It included not only descriptions of newly discovered evidence, but reinterpretations of previously known evidence. The presentation of "new" evidence played an important role in legitimating the exonerations. For example, Frank Lee Smith was exonerated by DNA tests 11 months after he died of cancer on death row. During his appeals, the *Sun Sentinel* reported that he was "stalling" his execution (Bulfin, 1990). When he died, the paper referred to him as "one of Broward County's most heinous killers" and reported that he "found Shandra Whitehead asleep" and then raped and killed her (LaMendola, 2000). When the DNA results were released, the paper reported that the results "exonerated" him (O'Boye, McMahon and Friedberg, 2000). The DNA was not the only "new evidence" reported. The paper also reported that the police had suspected another man of the crime immediately after it was committed. This "new suspect" had been known for 15 years, yet was only reported after Smith's death and exoneration. The "new" suspect was also "the suspect in more than a dozen murders and about 150 rapes" (O'Boye, McMahan and Friedberg, 2000). The paper reported this development only after Smith's death, but the original defense attorney admitted evidence regarding this man at Smith's trial. The *Sun Sentinel* never mentioned him in 15 years of reports. After the DNA exonerated Smith and implicated the known rapist and suspected murderer, the paper ran an article on a retired police officer who "felt vindicated" by the DNA results. He had known "in his gut" that Smith was innocent (Friedberg, 2000).

Shareef Cousin's case also involved new evidence. After the Louisiana Supreme Court reversed his conviction and the prosecutor dropped the charges, the *Times-Picayune* reported "within weeks" of the murder "separate tips... gave police the license plate of a car seen fleeing the scene, and three names of individuals..." (Varney, 1999). Detectives reviewed the criminal records of these men and found that they each had a history of arrests for crimes similar to the one Cousin was charged with committing. For Thomas Kimbell, the "new" evidence was in the files of prosecutors. He won a new trial and an acquittal due to the revelation that one statement by one witness was incorrect. The witness had testified that she was talking to her sister-in-law (the victim) on the phone an hour before the woman and three children were found murdered. She told the jury that the victim had told her "I got to go, somebody just pulled up in the driveway" (Silver, 2000). In her first statement to police, however, she reported that the victim said she had to go because her husband "Jake" pulled into the driveway. "Jake" is also the witness' brother (Silver, 2000; Lash, 2002).

In addition to "new" evidence, a lack of evidence was also an important indicator of innocence. This was especially compelling when the crimes had produced physical evidence. In the case of Timothy Hennis case, a woman and two of her young children were stabbed repeatedly and the adult victim was sexually assaulted. Crime scene investigators found fingerprints, palm prints and blood that was not from any of the victims (Wilkie, 1989a). When Hennis was acquitted the paper reported "that the state had no physical evidence linking Hennis to the murders." It also reported that the state was guilty of "ignoring evidence that implicated suspects other than Hennis." These statements were compelling indicators of Hennis' innocence (Wilkie, 1989a). In Joseph Burrows' case, only the alleged accomplice's "blood was found at the murder scene, and no physical evidence was ever found linking Burrows... to the crime" (Rooney, 1996). The cases against Albert Burrell and Michael Graham fell apart after the Louisiana Attorney General's office investigated the situation and reported a "total lack of physical evidence" tying either of the defendants to the crime (Guarisco, 2001a).

Reinterpretations of old evidence were also important to presenting the defendants as innocent of the charges. The reinterpretations were not necessarily expert opinions, they simply involved describing a situation differently or providing more detail that functioned to question the reliability of a witness or the credibility of evidence. While reports in numerous cases fit this pattern, those in Albert Burrell's, Michael Graham's, and Carl Lawson's are particularly demonstrative. Burrell and Graham were alleged accomplices in a double homicide, though it was only revealed after their exonerations that they did not know one another prior to their arrests. The only coverage of their separate trials were reports of their convictions and death sentences. When Graham was sentenced to death, *The Advocate* (1987) briefly summarized the case against him. The summary included the fact that "the star prosecution witness" testified that Graham had confessed to him when they were both in jail. The alleged confession included the fact that one victim "had been shot under the eye, a detail never revealed to the press." It also reported that Burrell's ex-wife had testified that she saw him with the male victim's wallet and Social Security card "the night of the murders" (*The Advocate*, 1987).

Unlike any other case in this population, it was representatives of the Attorney General's Office (who had assumed prosecutorial duties) that prompted the release of Graham and Burrell. The AG's report indicated that the case against them "should never have been brought to Grand Jury" (Guarisco, 2000). Further, the investigation revealed that the jailhouse informant or "star witness" had "an undisclosed history of mental illness..." and "he entered a plea deal... but prosecutors didn't tell the defense about it." The crime occurred in 1986, yet *The Advocate's* first mention of any problems with the case appeared in 2001 in the form of a series that explored the case. This three-part expose included a comment about the "star witness" from the man who was the county jailer in 1986. He said "if his lips moved, he was lying" (Baughman and Guarisco, 2001a). The second report in the series indicated that the witness was called "Lyin' Wayne" but had still been able to convince prosecutors "on several occasions" that other inmates had confessed to him "to cut better deals for himself" (Baughman and Guarisco, 2001b). This report also explained that Burrell's ex-wife had recanted her testimony and said that she had lied "to help her get custody of her son." There were countless other issues involved in this case, including witnesses lying to protect loved ones who were suspects, numerous witness recantations, and blood found at the scene that did not match the victims', Graham's, or Burrell's.

Carl Lawson's case also exemplifies the significance of reinterpreted evidence. Lawson was arrested for the murder of the son of his common law wife. During his trial it was reported that he left his "calling card – footprints" at the murder scene (Bosworth, 1990). The article described the evidence against Lawson, his relationship to the victim, his motive, and prior threats he allegedly made. All of this information was presented as undeniable fact. It was only after a jury acquitted him that the *St. Louis Post-Dispatch* reported that Lawson left his footprint near the child's body when he and "dozens of friends and family members" searched for and found the child. Only then did they mention that "dozens of people had walked through the crime scene." Only then did they report that the same witnesses told the police that Lawson was still sleeping when someone realized the child was missing (*St. Louis Post-Dispatch*, 1998). The additional information provided in the exoneration accounts painted a portrait of the story that was significantly different from what was described during the trial. The presence of this additional information, and the tone it created, functioned to legitimize the exonerations and delegitimize the death penalty.

The acceptance of error by system functionaries also offered significant credibility to the exonerations of these defendants. This does not mean that individual prosecutors or police officers admitted their role in convicting an innocent person, but that actions of prosecutors and/or police departments indicated their belief in the defendants' innocence. For example, when the *Times-Picayune* reported new evidentiary developments in Shareef Cousin's case, the developments were supported by this opening paragraph: "From the beginning, Shareef Cousin's attorneys said police had the wrong man. On Friday, the New Orleans Police Department tacitly concluded that might be right" (Varney, 1999). In Graham's and Burrell's cases, the fact that it was the Attorney General's Office's investigation that led to their release certainly legitimated the claims that were made.

Timothy Hennis' acquittal also benefited from law enforcement acceptance of the possibility that he was innocent. Immediately following the acquittal the District Attorney was "not aware that there are grounds for" reopening the investigation. He also indicated that he and representatives from the sheriff's department thought "from day one" that Hennis was guilty and that "there was no indication of any other suspect" (Barrett, 1989). One week later, the South Carolina Bureau of Investigation announced that it would "begin an immediate review" of the case due to "reports during the closing days of the trial that indicated someone else may have killed the Eastburns" (Barnes, 1989). This revelation came the same day the paper reported that Hennis, defense attorneys, the sheriff and police departments had all received letters from "Mr. X" which said "I murdered the Eastburns. I did the crime, Hennis is doing the time" (Wilkie, 1989b). Additionally, the exonerations were legitimized by articles under headlines like "Probe Continues; No Arrest in Ronda Morrison Murder" (Stewart, 1993b) and "Murder Probe is Active" (Handley, 1993b). Significantly, however, most cases contained no reports of law enforcement efforts to reopen, reassess, or reinvestigate the crimes.

The naming of new suspects also legitimized the notion that these defendants were not guilty. For example, Ray Krone was exonerated by DNA tests after his first conviction (Dodd, 1995), but the reports continued to present him as guilty based on bite mark evidence. It was only after his second conviction that DNA testing not only exonerated him, but established another suspect that Krone was presented as innocent of the murder. When this occurred, the presentation changed considerably. It was reported that "the DNA testing revealed that saliva... belonged not to Krone, but to" a man in prison "for an unrelated sex crime" (DeFalco and Wagner, 2002). The naming of another suspect also substantiated Robert Miller's claims. Despite the fact that DNA had excluded Miller and included another suspect, the prosecutor repeatedly said the DNA tests only proved Miller did not act alone. Eventually, when the state actually charged the other suspect and dropped charges against Miller, protestations by the prosecutor no longer appeared in the reports. The paper simply reported that Miller "was released from prison on DNA evidence" (Baldwin, 2001). Unfortunately for the new suspect, this statement was followed by "DNA test on semen from both rapes linked Lott to the crimes (Baldwin, 2001).

Gary Gauger also benefited from charges being filed against someone else. He had been convicted and sent to death row for the murders of his parents. The Illinois Supreme Court reversed the conviction based on lack of probable cause and excluded Gauger's confession. The fact that Gauger had confessed to these murders was reported in every article about his case. The prosecutors appealed the decision but lost and Gauger was released, though the state filed a motion "that would allow the charges to be reinstated if sufficient evidence is found" (Mount, 1996). He was released in October, 1996. In June 1997 the U.S. Attorney in Milwaukee, Wisconsin announced that members of the Outlaws motorcycle gang had been charged with the murders of Gauger's parents (Quintanilla and Murphy, 1997). Incidentally, the prosecutor was aware of the Wisconsin investigation in "early 1996" (Starks, 1997) but continued to fight Gauger's release.

OVERVIEW

As the cases described above indicate, the legitimation of the exonerations functioned to delegitimize the death penalty. The legitimation of capital punishment requires that members of society view the process as accurate and the defendants as guilty. The fact that mistakes were made and innocent people were sent to death row delegitimixed the punishment. The script changes in these death penalty cases presented a serious potential legitimacy crisis for the system. If left unchecked, these exonerations could have led to a true crisis. The reports of these changes, however, simultaneously functioned to relegitimize the death penalty. As a result, the socio-cultural system is attempting to mitigate the legitimacy crisis.

CHAPTER 7

Relegitimizing Capital Punishment

The articles that appeared after the canonical events overwhelmingly functioned to relegitimize the death penalty. Regardless of how the exoneration was presented, it required the relegitimation of capital punishment. A legal technicality that freed a guilty defendant presented a legitimacy crisis for the state, but so did the fact that an innocent person was sentenced to death. The release of someone from death row delegitimized capital punishment, but the reports of the exonerations consistently functioned to relegitimize the death penalty as public policy. This was accomplished in two primary ways. First, the exonerations were presented as anomalies with little connection to other exonerations or problems with the system. In other words, the newspapers' analyses of the situation employed a case specific approach. This technique was used when exonerations were presented as legitimate responses and as technicalities that freed guilty defendants. Second, the exonerations of innocent defendants were presented as evidence that the capital punishment system worked as it should. Quite simply, the fact that an innocent person was not executed was lauded as a success for the criminal justice system.

A CASE SPECIFIC APPROACH

The articles that appeared after the onset of the canonical events tended to explore the issue as case specific. They focused on the actions of characters in the particular case to determine what led to the problem. It is important to note that the "problem" was not necessarily a "wrongful conviction." The problem depended on the context of the article. If a review court had ordered a defendant's release, the "problem" was the basis for the court's ruling. When a particular piece of evidence was instrumental in an acquittal, the "problem" was the evidence and how its usefulness to the state had changed. When a witness recanted, the "problem" was the witness. The "problem" was rarely examined as it related to other capital convictions or exonerations. This approach was similar to the media's approach to crime in general. It is rare that crime reports include macro explanations; instead, the media tends to focus on individual criminals.

The notion of a case specific approach had two characteristics. First, the analyses of these cases tended to blame someone or something for the problem. This was true in the "technicality" cases and the "innocence" cases. Second, the articles rationalized the wrongful convictions by including negative information about the defendant. This technique was primarily used in cases that presented the exonerations as legitimate responses. Essentially, these articles indicated that this could not happen to just anyone. In taking a case specific approach, the exoneration reports avoided a presentation of systemic problems inherent in capital punishment policy.

IMPUTING BLAME

The first characteristic of the case specific approach was assigning blame. Forty-four percent (n=102) of wave five accounts blamed someone for the error. The recipients of blame differed considerably based on the way the exoneration was presented. The articles that presented the exonerations as legal technicalities that freed guilty defendants tended to blame review courts. In doing so, the articles indicated that review courts were overly concerned with the rights of criminals. When Joseph Green was acquitted following a bench trial because "the courts have suppressed all the evidence" the prosecutor went on to say: "courts taking it upon themselves and away from juries to decide is the problem in the case" (Hutchens and Fischer, 2000). The prosecutor in Steven Smith's case indicated that he disagreed with the Supreme Court's decision. "The Supreme Court had the option of sending this case back for trial. We think it should have done that instead of, in effect, trying the case itself without witnesses" (Armstrong and Lighty, 1999). When Larry Osborne was acquitted at retrial the prosecutor said evidentiary limits placed by the Kentucky

Supreme Court's ruling "made it very difficult for us to present enough evidence to convince a jury" (White, 2002). Similarly, when the Nebraska Supreme Court's ruling forced prosecutors to drop charges against Jeremy Sheets the prosecutor said "it is sad and unfortunate that the status of the evidence is changed by this court ruling, and that prevents us from bringing the truth to a jury" (Morton, 2001).

Other articles that presented the exonerations as technicalities that freed guilty defendants primarily blamed individual prosecutors. In the case of Robert Hayes the prosecutor was blamed for "prosecuting so many questionable cases" (Holland and Friedberg, 2000). The case of Clarence Dexter differed considerably from the others. The prosecutors were forced to drop charges against Dexter when they lost evidence they intended to present at the retrial. As a result, it was the victim's family that made the statements blaming prosecutors for the "injustice." In subsequent accounts, the victim's brother said "they're letting him out because they lost the evidence... someone has to be held responsible" (Williams, 1999a; Williams, 1999b; Rice, 1999). Essentially, in blaming review courts for the reversals and acquittals system functionaries were able to deflect attention from their weak cases and their overzealousness capital prosecutions.

The articles that presented the exonerations as legitimate responses also assigned blame. In fact, 50% (n=84) of these reports blamed someone. The primary difference between the two presentations was that the technicality cases blamed the system and the innocence cases blamed third parties or individual system functionaries. In the innocence cases that assigned blamed, 24% (n=40) blamed prosecutors, 30% (n=48) blamed witnesses, 12% (n=20) blamed police, five percent (n=8) blamed defense attorneys, and remarkably, five percent (n=9) blamed the defendant.

It is important to note that 46 articles blamed more than one person. For example, blame was tossed around like a hot potato when DNA exonerated Frank Smith after his death. First, the police blamed eyewitnesses. The Broward Sheriff's office spokesperson indicated that when the child was murdered police "immediately" suspected the known rapist. Yet, they "showed his photo" to eyewitness and "they did not pick him out" (O'Boye, McMahon, and Friedberg, 2000). The former detective who was "vindicated" by Smith's exoneration blamed his fellow police officers. He said "I knew Eddie Lee Mosley did that crime" but "they just wouldn't believe me at the time" (Friedberg, 2000). Further, Smith's family blamed an eyewitness who "later recanted and said she was pressured by police" (O'Boye, McMahon and Friedberg, 2000).

The blame in Smith's case extended beyond those responsible for the wrongful conviction. Because Smith had spent 14 years on death row, individuals were also deemed responsible for the fact that the DNA testing was only performed after his death. Defense attorneys blamed prosecutors for not allowing the tests. "They [prosecutors] have known since 1989 that the one person who identified Mr. Smith had recanted, but they fought us" (McMahon and Tzortzis, 2000). Prosecutors blamed defense attorneys and even the Florida Supreme Court. A prosecutor said "defense attorneys share the blame for not exonerating Smith before his death because they did not rush his appeal" (McMahon and Tzortzis, 2000). Further, the prosecutors said that he "complied with case law" because the Florida Supreme Court "still bans DNA testing in post-conviction cases" (McMahon and Tzortzis, 2000). The victim's aunt, however, brought some levity to the argument. She asked "a child is dead and you have to fight about it?" (McMahon and Tzortzis, 2000).

In other cases the blame was just as direct, though not as widely dispersed. For example, the *Tulsa World* consistently indicated that Greg Wilhoit was wrongfully convicted because his attorney did not "challenge the bite-mark evidence" during his trial (Braun, 1993). Other cases reserved blame for alleged accomplices and witnesses who committed perjury. For example, in Joseph Burrows' case the judge blamed Burrows' alleged accomplice, who was also wrongfully convicted, for "perverting the system with your perjury" (Rooney, 1996). The *Chicago Tribune* blamed a jailhouse informant by saying "his word, and little more, put Manning on Death Row" (Mills and Armstrong, 1999a). *The Decatur Daily* blamed "witnesses... who cut deals with authorities" for the wrongful conviction of Gary Drinkard (Marsh, 2001).

In the cases of Albert Burrell and Michael Graham blame was directed at the police, prosecutors, and witnesses. A defense attorney for the two said "gross misconduct by police and prosecutors" was "fully responsible for basically railroading these guys" (Guarisco, 2001b). The series of reports that examined the wrongful convictions of

Graham and Burrell concluded that witnesses lied, were unreliable, and that the prosecutor allowed their testimony despite these issues. The series clearly indicated that the prosecutor knew that the witnesses were providing false testimony. In short, one of the defense attorneys summed up the blame game:

> It's not a mistake, it's not a case that went through the cracks. This is a case where government officials - state employees - manufactured evidence to convict two innocent people (Baughman and Guarisco, 2001c; see also 2001a; 2001b).

The victims' family, however, held a different opinion. The male victim's brother blamed the judge for throwing out the convictions. He concluded "a woman shouldn't be a judge" (Baughman and Guarisco, 2001c).

Lastly, some of the articles actually blamed the defendants for their own wrongful convictions. This was an issue when defendants had allegedly confessed to police. For example, Ronald Jones shared the blame with police and the judge. Jones allegedly confessed to the rape and murder of the victim and prosecutors refused to drop charges for two years after DNA exonerated him (Hill, 1999). The prosecutor indicated that his reluctance to release Jones from custody was based on the fact that "Jones confessed to killing" the victim (Martin, 1997). Jones and his defense attorneys blamed the police, saying he confessed because police beat him "until I just couldn't take it no more" (Mills and Armstrong, 1999b). Incidentally, the *Chicago Tribune* also blamed the judge for his "resistance" to the DNA testing. For example, when defense attorneys asked the judge to allow DNA tests he replied "what issue could possibly be resolved by DNA testing?" (Mills and Armstrong, 199b). When the same judge later came under fire for calling defense attorneys "idiots" Jones' attorney reflected on his refusal to allow the tests. "It was difficult for us to understand why someone who was so convinced of Mr. Jones' guilt, as the judge clearly was, would fight us so hard on the testing" (Mills and Armstrong, 2000).

Gary Gauger was also blamed for his wrongful conviction. His alleged confession to police was the focus of numerous reports after the Illinois Supreme Court ruled that his statements were "fruits of an illegal arrest" (Quintanilla and Mount, 1996). The prosecutor quickly pointed out: "the court did not say his confession was coerced out of him" (Quintanilla, 1996). When members of the Outlaws motorcycle gang were charged with the murder the paper reported that Gauger was convicted "largely based on an alleged confession" (Quintanilla and Murphy, 1997). Even one of the bikers who had killed the couple blamed Gauger. During his testimony he reported that when Gauger "had confessed... I recall" the other biker "and myself saying, 'that's great'" (Starks, 1999a). Finally, when Gauger sued county officials over his wrongful conviction, the attorney who represented the officials said "our position has been and remains that Gary Gauger was prosecuted because he had told the police that he killed his parents" (Starks, 1999b). In essence, the articles were able to deflect attention from systemic problems in the capital punishment system by placing blame for the circumstances on an individual. They also, however, used an additional technique.

BAD THINGS HAPPEN TO BAD PEOPLE

The articles also avoided blaming the system or the policy for the problems by presenting the defendants as bad people. In doing so, the reports informed their audience that wrongful convictions only happened to bad people. This technique was used in 17% (n=40) of the wave five accounts. Prior felony convictions were the primary focus of these accounts. For example, following Joseph Green's acquittal *The Gainesville* reminded readers that Green had

> once spent three years in prison for second-degree murder and 2½ years in prison for battery of a correctional officer. Green's record also shows charges of robbery, assault, heroin possession and fraud (Hutchens and Fischer, 2000).

Steven Smith "had been convicted of two other murders before being charged" with the murder that sent him to death row (Armstrong and Lighty, 1999). Similarly, Frank Lee Smith "had a bad record, there's no question." He had "an extensive criminal background dating back to his teenage years, when he killed two people" (O'Boye, McMahon and Friedberg, 2000). Joseph Burrows was "ornery," a "troublemaker," and had a "criminal history" that proved "he couldn't follow the rules of society" (Rooney, 1994b). Presenting the defendants as different from others in society was also achieved by describing other kinds of negative behaviors. For example, Alfred Rivera was a "drug dealer" who admitted that "he had drug dealings" with the victims (Stolberg, 2000). Thomas Kimbell was a "cocaine addict" (Lash, 2002). Sabrina Butler, who was convicted and then exonerated in the murder of her 9 month-old son admitted "to hitting her baby once in the stomach because he was getting on her nerves" (Mitchell, 1995). This approach is similar to the media's overall approach to crime reporting. It tends to take individual rather than macro approaches to reports of crime and criminality.

Other accounts focused on the fact that the defendant would remain in prison on other charges despite being exonerated in the murder cases. When Ronald Jones was acquitted by DNA evidence, he "remained at Cook County Jail" because he had escaped from "a work-release program in 1980" while serving "a 5-year sentence for robbery" and was fugitive at the time of his arrest on murder charges (Mills and Armstrong, 1999). Similarly, when Steve Manning was exonerated, the *Chicago Tribune* reminded readers that he was "the former leader of an underworld robbery gang." The article went on to inform the reader that:

> The ruling does not mean Manning will go free. He is serving a natural life sentence in Missouri for kidnapping a Kansas City drug figure and holding him for ransom in 1984 (Parsons, 1998).

These types of negative descriptions about exonerated defendants functioned to relegitimize the death penalty. They solidified the criminal/non-criminal dichotomy. In early waves, negative representations of defendants functioned to legitimize the death penalty for a particular crime. In waves four and five these characterizations functioned to relegitimize capital punishment in the wake of delegitimizing forces.

The newspapers consistently explored the problematic issues in these cases in a way that indicated to readers that the problems were case specific. They achieved this representation by assigning blame to an individual or review court, and by characterizing the defendants as bad people who were essentially being punished for other behaviors. The articles also, however, relegitimized the death penalty by indicating that the exonerations were proof the system works.

THE SYSTEM WORKS

Wave five accounts also relegitimized the death penalty by presenting the exonerations as proof the system worked as it should. This technique was not used as often as expected. It was completely absent from articles that presented the exonerations as technicalities and was used in only 11% (n=19) of the articles that presented them as legitimate responses. It was present in only 8% (n=19) of all wave five accounts. When it was used, however, it was primarily achieved through statements of politicians and system functionaries, though others occasionally supported this notion.

The statements from politicians were predominately in response to attempts to amend or suspend death penalty statutes following an exoneration. For example, when the Arizona legislature debated a law that would allow juries to sentence defendants to death, one representative said "I just want to remind people that 12 folks found Ray Krone guilty" (Fischer, 2002). Another indicated that Krone's case does not mean the state should eliminate the death penalty because "I think it [the system] worked for Ray Krone - eventually" (Fischer, 2002). In response to Illinois' ninth exoneration attorneys and some lawmakers called for a moratorium on executions. A spokesperson for then Governor George Ryan said "while we support efforts to improve our system, we disagree with the contention that it's broken" (*Champaign-Urbana News Gazette*, 1997).

Unlike Illinois, North Carolina had experienced only two death row exonerations in a 23-year period. The situation in Illinois, however, did prompt North Carolina to examine its capital punishment system. Then Governor Jim Hunt was "confident that we have not executed anyone who was not guilty. Our system is fair and efficient" (Stolberg, 2000). The deputy attorney general in charge of capital cases reiterated the notion that the current system of capital punishment works by saying:

With the multiple levels of appellate reviews afforded death-penalty cases, and the high degree of scrutiny they receive at each level, I do not see how an innocent person could or would be convicted in North Carolina (Stolberg, 2000).

Following the release of Michael Graham and Albert Burrell the Louisiana legislature debated a moratorium on executions. The director of the District Attorney's Association said "no innocent people have been put to death, and courtroom strategies exist to give defendants a full hearing on appeal" (McClain, 2001). The report indicated that the debate quickly became less about the possibility of executing innocent people and more about the fact that "swift justice taking place is not happening in Louisiana." In other words, the only problem with Louisiana's capital punishment system is that it doesn't execute anyone fast enough. One representative argued that "we do need to limit the appeals" and he was submitting a bill to that end (McClain, 2001). Another indicated that "legal appeals are the key reason for how long it takes to carry out executions" (McClain, 2001). Incidentally, Burrell and Graham spent 13 years on death row. Burrell came within 17 days of being executed. Their appeals were consistently denied.

Other politicians who spoke out in support of the system also tended to focus on the notion that the system worked as it should, or that lengthy appeals represent the primary problem with capital punishment. For example, after William Nieves was exonerated the Pennsylvania legislature considered a bill that would improve the indigent defense system. Nieves testified before the legislature and urged them to enact the legislation. A spokesperson for then Governor Tom Ridge indicated that not only is legal representation "adequate" in capital cases, but the only problem with the death penalty rests with the lengthy appeals. He said: "It is an inarguable fact that in every instance where a convicted murderer wanted to thwart the death penalty, they were able to" (Fitzgerald, 2000). Following a public demonstration in opposition to the death penalty, the same spokesperson said: "If there's any glaring problem with the Pennsylvania death penalty, it's that convicted murderers have mostly escaped their punishment" (Blanchard, 2001).

Not all of these comments were in the context of efforts to modify death penalty statutes. Following Walter McMillian's exoneration, a

U.S. Senator from Alabama delivered a speech in McMillian's home town. He indicated that the case "showed that the Alabama criminal-justice system is working well" (Montgomery, 1993). He acknowledged that McMillian had "suffered a great deal for being in prison" but "when the new evidence was there, the Alabama court of [Criminal] Appeals reversed and turned him loose. It wasn't a federal court that did it" (Montgomery, 1993). The senator's comments indicate that he was unfamiliar with the facts of the case. In fact, Alabama review courts consistently denied McMillian's appeals until numerous problems with the conviction were exposed by the report by *60 Minutes*. Further, McMillian's case was remanded for retrial and the prosecutor dropped the charges. The review court did not "turn him loose."

A few articles simply recognized the fallibility of the system. When Frank Lee Smith was exonerated after he died of cancer on death row, the prosecutor who had fought DNA testing said:

> This doesn't shake my belief in the death penalty. We're in a system where guilty people go free, and sometimes innocent people are incarcerated. This is a human institution, and we pray that mistakes like this aren't made (O'Boye, McMahon and Friedberg, 2000).

Following Alfred Rivera's exoneration, a gubernatorial candidate said the "order for a new trial vindicated the system's ability to correct its own errors" but a law professor from the University of North Carolina disagreed. He summed up the reality of death penalty retention.

> There is no criminal-justice system in the world that has 100% accuracy.... One of the prices we have to pay if we want the death penalty is that we are going to execute some innocent people. There is just no way to avoid that (Stolberg, 2000).

In sum, the fact that politicians and system functionaries felt compelled to respond to the exonerations is indicative of the legitimacy crisis the system faces from capital exonerations. While the statements were somewhat diverse, the tie that binds them is their attempts to relegitimize the system of capital punishment. There was, however, one other issue in wave five accounts that deserves attention.

IGNORING THE ISSUE

While wave five accounted for 22% (n=231) of all reports, the exonerations were often ignored or quickly forgotten. The mean number of articles per case in wave five was eight. While seven cases had 15 or more articles that either focused on the exonerations directly or mentioned them, 12 cases had less than five articles that mentioned the exoneration, and three involved only one report. Essentially, some newspapers relegitimized the death penalty by ignoring the exonerations. In others, the context in which the exonerations were mentioned functioned to relegitimize the capital punishment system.

Relegitimation by context involved a brief mention of an exoneration in an article that focused on a recent execution, another death verdict, some other death row development, compensation efforts, or even stories on "infamous crimes." For example, nine years after Timothy Hennis was acquitted of a triple murder, an article appeared in the *Fayetteville Observer Times* (1998) under the headline "Notorious Crimes." The article offered brief descriptions of several high-profile crimes in the community. It identified the date and location of crime that sent Hennis to death row and then said:

Hennis... is convicted of the murders in July 1986 and spends 845 days on death row before the state Supreme Court overturns his conviction and orders a new trial. Nearly two years later, a Wilmington jury acquits him (*Fayetteville Observer*, 1998).

The article goes on to describe other cases and the fact that several of the "notorious criminals" remained under death sentences. Articles of this type relegitimated the death penalty by reporting other death verdicts and by minimizing the exonerations.

In other cases it was the state's reactions to defendants' attempts to be compensated for their wrongful convictions that functioned to relegitimize the death penalty. For Walter McMillian, the state legislature simply refused to vote on a bill that would have compensated him for his years on death row (*Monroe Journal*, 1993b).

Later, the Monroe County Commission also refused his request for compensation (Montgomery and Stewart, 1993). When Albert Burrell and Michael Graham sought compensation for their 13 years on death row, the director of the Louisiana District Attorneys Association said "do we want to hold the state liable for every mistake made in the criminal justice system?" (Guarisco, 2001b). Further, in wake of Burrell's and Graham's exonerations the Louisiana legislature debated two separate bills that would have offered them compensation, but neither bill made it out of committee (Guarisco, 2001c). Additionally, when Joseph Burrow's sought compensation, the county finally settled. They did so because "it was less costly than going to trial" (Monson, 1997).

One important characteristic of these types of accounts was the change in their descriptions of events. When Shareef Cousin was exonerated, the reports of his case overwhelmingly indicated that he was innocent, the prosecutors were guilty of misconduct, and the police had failed in their investigation. Three years later, in a report of Cousin's efforts to sue the prosecutor the article did not describe the allegations of misconduct, but it did define the concept of immunity. The importance of this report lies in its description of the exoneration. It reports that the prosecutor "dropped charges against Cousin, saying it couldn't win again but calling Cousin guilty as originally charged" (Filosa, 2002). The report further stated that "prosecutors relied on eyewitness testimony" but did point out that "no physical evidence" connected Cousin to the crime.

While there were other reports of other defendants' attempts at compensation, these exemplify the primary contradiction. When the exonerations first occurred, blame was passed around. The articles tended to focus on the individual who was responsible. When it came time to hold someone accountable, the articles changed their presentations. Essentially, the reports of defendants' efforts to receive some monetary compensation were used to relegitimize the death penalty. They shifted focus to the excuses used when the issues were first revealed. They focused on the evidence that convicted the defendants and they presented the information in a way that indicated any rational person could have reached the same conclusion about the defendant's culpability.

Other post-exoneration reports functioned to relegitimize the death penalty by reporting on various death row developments. For example, in Robert Miller's case, a jury sentenced the new defendant to death (Godfrey, 2001). The last mention of Albert Burrell or Michael Graham was in the context of a reduction in the number of executions in Louisiana (*The Advocate*, 2002). The last mention of Timothy Hennis' exoneration was in the context of a pending execution in North Carolina (Woolverton, 2001).

The significance of these issues is that they relegitimize capital punishment by indicating that the exoneration was not enough to stop executions. They connoted a general acceptance of the potential for error in the system. In doing so, they reinforced the notion that the current system of capital punishment functions in way that detects error. That it is fair and just. Essentially, when error is detected, the defendant is released. No harm, no foul.

CHAPTER 8

Contributions and Conclusions

The United States, as a late capitalist society, is in a constant state of crisis prevention (Habermas, 1975). The criminal justice system, as part of the socio-cultural system, is but one of a multitude of state functions that must always be in careful balance. This balance exists only when the public views the system's actions and policies as legitimate. Any perception of unfairness, error, or ineffectiveness presents a legitimation crisis. It is when the public recognizes or politicizes these limits and problems that a true crisis occurs (Habermas, 1975). Death row exonerations present a potential legitimacy crisis to the system of capital punishment and the criminal justice system. This crisis, however, has been successfully handled by the state, and to date a true legitimacy crisis has been avoided. The public's internalization of the problem and the politicization of the issue, however, are indicative of the fact that the state is facing a true crisis due to capital exonerations. The legitimacy of capital punishment continues to erode with each new exoneration. Capital exonerations generate reaction, which exacerbates the potential for crisis. The exonerations themselves are not the only catalyst for the crisis. It is the interaction of the characteristics of the cases and the exonerations that present a challenge to the legitimacy of capital punishment and the criminal justice system. Through content analysis I was able to explore the characteristics of the cases, coverage, and sources of information. As a result, I have contributed to the literature on capital sentencing, newspaper crime coverage, and death row exonerations.

CONTENT ANALYSIS CONTRIBUTIONS

Despite the small population and the limitations of the data, the results of the content analysis lend some support to other research that has been conducted on decision-making in capital cases, sources in crime stories, and story salience. This analysis revealed that story salience was impacted by victim and offender characteristics. Specifically, cases involving white victims received more coverage than those with minority victims. My analysis supports the research of Johnstone, Hawkins, and Michener (1994), Chermak (1998a), Wilbanks (1984); Pritchard and Hughes (1997), and Sorenson, Manz, and Berk, (1998) among others. The cases with child and multiple victims received more coverage than other cases. Essentially, this research supports the notion that the media focuses on the sensational. I also found that cases with white defendants received more press than those involving minorities, which supports the findings of Chermak (1998b) and Paulsen (2003).

Additionally, these newspapers relied on state sources for information. Sigal (1973) and Chermak (1995a; 1995b), among others, found that print media outlets depend heavily on state sources for information. They revealed that more than half of all sources in articles about crime are police, prosecutors, or other representatives of the state. This data supports their findings. This analysis revealed that the newspapers that covered the crimes, trials, post-conviction efforts, and exonerations of these defendants relied heavily on state sources. This dependence was true regardless of geography, newspaper size, or wave. During every stage of the case, the reports focused on the presentation of the state's message. The only exception to this was wave five. The exoneration reports included information from defense sources to present a more balanced effort. The content of what was reported was impacted by the reliance on state sources for information. The crimes were presented as heinous, the defendants were presented in a negative way, and the defendants were presented as guilty of the crimes. These themes were directly tied to the presence of state sources and the absence of defense sources in the articles.

The analysis of the characteristics of the cases also supports the findings of other researchers. Specifically, research has consistently revealed that the interaction of victim and defendant race is the leading factor in the filing of capital charges and seeking the death penalty (see Baldus, Woodworth, and Pulaski, 1990; Keil and Vito, 1995; Sorensen and Wallace, 1995a, 1995b; Thomson, 1997; Sorensen and Wallace, 1999). This analysis revealed that half the cases with African-American defendants involved white victims. Research also indicates that cases with white defendants usually require more aggravating factors than those involving black defendants (Baldus, Woodworth, and Pulaski, 1990). In this analysis, cases with white defendants involved multiple aggravating factors. Researchers have also determined that cases with white defendants are capitally charged only when the crimes are particularly heinous (Thomson, 1997; Sorensen and Wallace, 1999). This analysis supports that to some degree. The crimes charged against white defendants were more likely to involve knives and multiple injuries than the cases involving minorities, especially African-Americans.

The primary issue that has been raised by these results relates to the functioning of the criminal justice system. These articles revealed that changes of venue were rare, yet many of these cases were high profile and received much publicity. The fact that venue changes were not sought or not granted is very problematic. It appears that conducting high-profile criminal trials in the jurisdiction in which the crime was committed was one factor that may have led to many of these wrongful convictions. This issue deserves further analysis.

Misconduct by system functionaries was also very problematic. The newspaper accounts and court rulings revealed that prosecutorial misconduct and judicial error were the most frequent reasons cited by review courts for overturning these convictions. The misconduct in these cases did not involve simple mistakes or errors in judgement. These cases involved contemplated, egregious actions on the part of prosecutors. These cases involved prosecutors who hid witnesses, withheld exculpatory evidence, suborned perjury, and coached witnesses. In sum, these cases were plagued by egregious prosecutorial misconduct. The patterns of prosecutorial misconduct revealed by this analysis support the findings of Miller-Potter (2002).

Additionally, the newspaper accounts and court decisions also revealed that judicial error was a factor in these wrongful convictions. As with prosecutors, the "errors" by judges were based on issues that first year law students would understand. As previously discussed, two judges in different states actually allowed uncross-examined testimony of dead witnesses. The right to cross-examine accusers is a fundamental right clearly outlined in the constitution, yet these judges allowed these statements entered as evidence. In addition to allowing testimony of dead people, judges in these cases allowed prosecutors to make statements to the juries about the lack of testimony by the defendant, excluded allowable alibi and other exculpatory evidence, and allowed evidence of prior criminal history. The most significant result gleaned from this data, however, was the fact that the defendants were convicted on so little evidence. Overwhelmingly these defendants were sent to death row with little or no evidence that they were actually involved in the crimes. Scientific evidence was present in only ten cases. Even this small percentage does not accurately portray the role science played in these cases. In some cases when scientific evidence was present it still did not indicate the guilt of the defendant. For example, at the first trial of Timothy Hennis, fibers from a piece of burned corduroy were entered as evidence in an attempt to link Hennis to the crime (Ruffin, 1986a). The state argued that the murderer had sat on a bed and left a "corduroy like impression" on a sheet. Despite the fact that the laboratory technician revealed that it was not possible to determine if the fabric from Hennis' home had made the impression, the fact that no blood was found in his car, home, or clothing, Hennis was convicted of a very brutal, very bloody, triple homicide. Further, Hennis was sent to death row despite the fact that fingerprints, a palm print, and blood found at the crime scene did not match his (Ruffin 1986b).

Greg Wilhoit and Ray Krone were sent to death row on the basis of bite mark evidence. This type of evidence is recognized as unreliable, yet two defendants were sent to death row on the combination of bite marks and circumstantial evidence. Other cases were just as troubling. Robert Lee Miller was arrested and convicted because the hair of a black male was found in the victim's bed. When police saw him walk through the neighborhood Miller, who is mentally challenged, told them he had a dream about the murders (Clay, 1987). Larry Osborne was convicted in part because a window was broken at the victims' home and glass fragments were found on his clothing (Taylor, 2001). It apparently did not matter to jurors, the prosecutor, or judge that the glass fragments did not come from the same source. These defendants were largely convicted on little more than circumstantial evidence.

Police and prosecutors in these cases consistently relied on circumstantial evidence to identify suspects and subsequently convict them. In fact, approximately half of these cases involved little more than circumstantial evidence. Many defendants were charged because they had been seen with the victim prior to the crime, or because they knew the victim. This was especially true of cases involving spouses and partners, but it was true for others as well. One case that is particularly troubling is that of Timothy Hennis, who was charged with the murders of a woman and two of her young children. The victim's husband was an Air Force captain who was about to be transferred to Great Britain. This pending move forced the family to give up their pet dog. The victim placed an advertisement in the local military newspaper and Hennis responded to the ad. He met the victim only one time when he picked up the dog. That was just two days before the murders (Krisher and Jones, 1985). When the crime was discovered, police began searching for the man who adopted the dog. Hennis willingly went to the police station, spent five hours under interrogation, and offered blood and hair samples. Despite the fact that the samples he provided exonerated him, going to the police was to his detriment. He was charged with the murders the same day (Krisher and Jones, 1985).

The overwhelming lack of evidence against these defendants lends support to research on capital juries. Research indicates that death qualified jurors are conviction-prone (Williams and McShane, 1990), and that they view the death penalty as mandatory upon conviction (Geimer and Amsterdam, 1987). Lack of evidence and the misrepresentation of evidence by state's witnesses is also indicative of a problem with judicial oversight. The fact that judges allow juries to render conviction verdicts and then sentence defendants to death in light of so little evidence is frightening. Judges do have discretion, and they maintain the power to invoke summary judgments. In fact, in the case of Ray Krone the judge was quoted as saying "although the court agrees with the jury's (guilty) verdict, the court is left with a residual or lingering doubt about the clear identity of the killer" (Ruggiero, 2002). Perhaps "lingering doubt" differs from "reasonable doubt." The fact that judges are willing to allow these miscarriages of justice in their courtrooms could be related to the fact that judges are mostly elected officials. This troubling issue deserves further attention. Ultimately, however, the primary significance of this research lies in the results of the narrative analysis.

NARRATIVE ANALYSIS CONTRIBUTIONS

The narrative portion of this project focused on the legitimation techniques in the reports of death penalty cases. The local newspapers analyzed herein provided the avenue through which the state was able to legitimize and relegitimize its social control agenda. Legitimation of the death penalty prior to the onset of the canonical events required the legitimation of the state's ability to punish. The death penalty is just one issue within the criminal justice system that functions to legitimate the state's crime control agenda. It offers the appearance of strong, effective state action. More importantly, it operates under the facade that the state is willing to take forceful action on behalf of public safety. This notion was supported by the findings of this analysis. Wave one accounts tended to present the crimes as public problems and the police as crime solvers. These two themes functioned to legitimate the subsequent actions taken by the state. The legitimation of a state's ability to use force against its citizens requires that the public view the use of force as being in their best interest. The reports analyzed herein functioned in that way. The articles that focused on the crimes presented them as public problems. The subsequent action, therefore, was legitimated because the crime itself was presented as threatening the moral order of a community.

Additionally, wave one accounts reinforced the state's crime control agenda by presenting the police as crime solvers and by relying on police for information about the crimes. Presenting the police as crime solvers reinforced the notion that the police are protectors of society and defenders of the law, rather than agents of social control. The reliance on police as sources of information about the crimes enabled the police to impart their crime control agenda on the public, and to present the police function in the best possible light. In short, the reports of the crimes for which these defendants were sent to death row functioned to legitimate the state's social control agenda.

The legitimation of capital punishment also requires presenting the crimes as particularly heinous and, therefore, deserving of the ultimate punishment. This hypothesis was also supported by the data. This legitimation technique was used in accounts prior to the onset of the canonical events. Waves one, two, and three consistently presented the crimes as particularly heinous events. Additionally, they presented the victims as particularly sympathetic individuals who had their positive, normative life experiences disrupted by violence. Doing so functioned to legitimize the necessity of punishment, the death penalty in a particular case, and capital punishment as public policy. Legitimation of the state's ability to punish further requires the establishment of defendant dangerousness. This postulate was also supported by the data. The newspaper accounts reporting the arrests of the defendants, their trials, and even post-exoneration accounts presented the defendants as different from the rest of society. Reports in early waves focused on the general negative characteristics and presented the defendants as "thugs," "violent career offenders," "anomalous killers," and "crazy killers." The reports consistently reinforced the notion that these defendants were not able to successfully function in a civil society. They were dregs who had been in and out of jails and prisons. They had been provided multiple opportunities to be rehabilitated and had failed. Presenting them in this way facilitated the state's ability to not only remove them from society, but to invoke the harshest penalty.

The significance of presenting the defendants as "evil" was further supported by the notion that the victims were "good." The early waves focused on the positive characteristics of the victims and the fact that their normative life experiences were disrupted by violence. In short, the victims were presented as being like other good people in society while the defendants were presented as being different. This dichotomous representation of the victims and defendants further legitimated the ultimate penalty for these crimes.

Presenting the defendants as bad people who were different from everyone else facilitated the notion that they were guilty of the crimes. When the focus was on the legitimation of the death penalty for a particular crime, the defendants were consistently presented as guilty. This representation, however, changed as the story evolved. When the exonerations were imminent, the guilty presentations decreased considerably, but the negative presentations continued. This served to legitimate the death penalty as public policy. In essence, it sent the message that wrongful convictions cannot happen to just anyone. It was a reminder that these were bad people who had prior experience with the criminal justice system. This message supports the state's social control agenda. It indicated that the defendants were law violators and their time on death row could be viewed as punishment for other deviant acts.

Legitimation of the death penalty for a defendant and as public policy also requires that the public accept it as fair and accurate. These notions were also present in the reports. The early waves reported information about the system's processing of defendants. In cases with a great deal of coverage, each hearing or court appearance was reported. Legal concepts were defined and trials were presented as adversarial events that were designed to actualize justice. After the canonical events, waves four and five focused on the post-conviction activities. They described legal arguments, the appeals process, and even indicated that too many appeals were available. The descriptions of appeals and the notion that too many exist, functioned to advance the veneer of procedural justice the state utilizes to legitimate the death penalty.

Prior to the canonical events, the newspapers overwhelmingly presented the system as accurate. The defendants were presented as guilty of the crimes and the reports described all the evidence that proved it. Any contradictory views of a defendant's guilt were downplayed. These views were presented as bizarre beliefs by family members or others who were unwilling to accept the overwhelming evidence of the defendant's guilt. Evidence that supported the states' cases was, however, provided much space in the articles and was very rarely questioned. Alleged confessions to jailhouse snitches, statements by alleged accomplices who turned out to be the culpable parties, shaky scientific evidence, and incredibly weak circumstantial evidence were all reported as proof of guilt. The integrity of these various forms of "evidence" and the motives of questionable witness were very rarely questioned in the early waves. This, however, evolved as cases began to fall apart and the stories changed.

The canonical events caused a dramatic shift in how the cases were presented to the public. For the first time in the metastories, the inaccuracy of the system became an issue. The defendants may not have been guilty. The state may have been wrong. An innocent person could have been executed. Capital exonerations expose the state's fallibility. They reveal the ineffectiveness of the criminal justice system. They raise questions of unethical behavior by system functionaries and the fundamental unfairness of the system. I hypothesized that these canonical events would lead to an alteration in the legitimation techniques, that the focus would change to the relegitimation capital punishment. This hypothesis was supported by the data. The exonerations of these defendants did lead to relegitimation efforts.

The results of this portion of the analysis support the research of Benford and Hunt (2003). The state utilized counterframing efforts after the canonical events. In fact, three of the four counterframing processes identified by Benford and Hunt (2003) were present in wave four and five accounts. Through the reports, state functionaries practiced "problem denial." They denied the existence of error until they were forced to by review courts. Secondly, state sources used "counter attributions." They blamed others for the underlying causes of the problem. Third, they practiced "counter prognoses" by recognizing the existence of a problem, but offered alternative solutions. Specifically, they often argued that the exonerations revealed the need for modification of the death penalty system. Unfortunately, the reports often indicated that the necessary changes should include a streamlined appeals process, or other changes that favored the state's efforts. Finally, the only counterframing technique not present in the reports were "attacks on collective character." While wave four and five articles and system functionaries attacked the character of individual defendants, they did not attempt to discredit defense attorneys, or anti-death penalty groups in a collective sense. In short, the local print media provided an outlet for the counterframing efforts of system functionaries following the canonical events.

These counterframing techniques were necessary because the exonerations required rehabilitative messages from the state. This was accomplished through media amplification of state explanations and excuses. Death row exonerations have the potential to create a fundamental legitimacy crisis, if for no other reason, because the state loses control of the story. Other voices are heard. The increased presence of other voices means that audience reaction could be less directed than in initial stages. Instead of audience anger being directed at an individual "criminal," it could have become directed at the policy. Essentially, the emergence of the canonical events posed a legitimacy crisis because the state lost its monopoly control of information about the story. Waves four and five were the only time in the metastories that defense sources were even close to being on par with state sources. The state was, however, able to mitigate the crisis through relegitimation efforts in exoneration accounts..

Exoneration reports consistently used a case specific approach in the examination of the cases. While the original crimes were presented as public problems, the exonerations were presented as individual problems. The crimes threatened civil society. The exonerations threatened one person. The case specific approach primarily involved blaming an individual person or institution for the error. Additionally, the reports reviewed the "strong" evidence against the defendants. This functioned to convey the idea that it was a true "error," that anyone would have believed the defendant was guilty. The combination of this happening to a bad person, because one person was to blame, and that anyone could have made the mistake, functioned to relegitimize the death penalty as public policy.

The relegitimation technique that was not used often as I expected, was presenting the exoneration as proof the system works. This was the focus of some accounts, though not to the degree anticipated. The articles that presented the exonerations in this way tended to revert to a discussion of the problems of due process. They posited that death row inmates have too much protection and that the system is overly concerned with the rights of criminals. This surprising characteristic also, however, functioned to relegitimize the death penalty. These reports informed their audiences that despite the years on death row, the denied appeals, and the protestations of innocence, the only problem with the death penalty is that it is not implemented quickly enough. Essentially, they offered reassurance that those in position to change death penalty statutes were not concerned by the exonerations. The public, therefore, should not be concerned either.

CONCLUSIONS

The data analyzed herein cannot determine what, if any, role the local print media played in these wrongful convictions. What it has revealed, however, is that commonalities existed in how these cases were presented. These patterns were true regardless of geography or newspaper size. Each legitimation and relegitimation technique that was present in these articles was advanced by a reliance on state sources. While some papers were worse than others, they all reported the state's messages. By presenting the state's messages, they facilitated the agenda building efforts of the police and prosecutors. The reports consistently failed to question the integrity of evidence that prosecutors described for them. They summarized evidence in a way that presented the state's theories as accurate accounts of the events. In doing so, they invariably reported "facts" that were eventually revealed to be incorrect. They consistently failed to question the accuracy of the information provided by the state. The relegitimation efforts, therefore, functioned not only to relegitimize the death penalty, but to relegitimize the newspaper and its reporting.

The articles frequently summarized or described "key" evidence presented by prosecutors, but rarely reported alternate explanations. Two articles exemplify the primary problem with the way these cases were presented throughout the metastories. When the *Chicago Tribune* reported Steve Manning's conviction, it stated that "jurors heard several tapes where Manning allegedly confessed to killing" the victim (Wilson, 1993). After Manning's exoneration the *Tribune* ran a scathing five-part series on capital sentencing in Illinois (see Mills and Armstrong, 1999). Part three of the series described Manning's "confession" differently:

> But when the tapes were played in court, there were no murder confessions. Dye's [a jailhouse informant] explanation: Manning's confessions were lost in two seconds-long gaps in the recordings (Mills and Armstrong, 1999).

It begs the question: was the reporter even in court when the tapes were played? The use of "allegedly" indicates that he was not. In that case, where did he get the information? The statement about the jury hearing confession tapes was not attributed to anyone in the article. It was simply reported as fact. Further, the trial report indicated that the "informant" was, at the time of the trial, in the federal witness protection program. It did not question his motives. It did not question the content of the tapes. Six years later, the exoneration report criticized the prosecution for using "such untrustworthy witnesses" and indicated that jailhouse informants "have little to lose by lying on the witness stand" (Mills and Armstrong, 1999).

This lone wave five article from one newspaper in a single case also exemplifies one of the most significant findings of this analysis. Wave five accounts were the most balanced articles in the metastories. The tone of the articles overwhelmingly questioned the convictions and the state's role in the mistakes, but they also presented the state's response. When the defendants were arrested, on trial, and convicted the papers gave far more attention to state theories than to defense theories or alibis. As a whole, the newspapers did not question the cases against the defendants until they were forced to by a change in the story. Only one reporter was instrumental in undermining the state's efforts. Peter Rooney at the *Champaign-Urbana News Gazette* investigated Joseph Burrows' conviction. His efforts eventually led to Burrows' release. After a series of exonerations in Illinois, the *Chicago Tribune* ran a vitriolic series that questioned both the application of capital punishment and its legitimacy as public policy. The other papers, however, did not. They discussed witness issues, evidentiary problems, and even issues relating to misconduct by system functionaries. They traced how mistakes were made in a particular case, but did not examine capital punishment as public policy.

The reports analyzed herein were not balanced, fair accounts. They overwhelmingly presented the situations in a way that was favorable to the state. The reports worked to legitimize the death penalty during every wave, even after the canonical events. Several of the papers ran post-exoneration articles that questioned the integrity of the case against the defendants, or asked "how did this happen?" These accounts did effectively undermine the legitimacy of capital punishment, but the information was reported in a way that functioned to relegitimize it by focusing on the issue as case specific and placing blame. Some reports blamed individual system functionaries for the mistake. Others blamed police departments for shoddy investigations. Some questioned the use of certain types of informants, but in the end, very few questioned the death penalty as public policy.

In sum, the reports of these crimes and trials were little more than presentations of the state's messages. The articles focused on the state's theories of the crimes and presented the defendants as guilty. During each wave, the state was provided an avenue for legitimating and even relegitimating its social control agenda. The reports of the crimes tended to focus on how they disrupted the moral order of a community.

The reports of arrest, trials, and appeals were designed to restore the community's moral order by reporting that justice was being served. The reports of exonerations worked to strengthen the legitimacy of the system of social control that erred in the first place. These dynamics in the local print media coverage of these capital cases do fundamental violence to the concept and reality of justice.

References

Advocate, The. (1987). "21-year-old sentenced to death." May 24. B9.

Advocate, The. (1991). "Death row inmate loses appeal." January 22. D9.

Advocate, The. (2002). "Number of executions down in 2001 none executed in LA." January 3. B3.

Altheide, D. L. (1976). *Creating reality: How TV news distorts events.* Thousand Oaks, CA: Sage.

Altheide, D. L. (2002). *Creating Fear: News and the Construction of Crisis.* Hawthorne, NY: Aldine De Gruyter.

Anderson, J. (1992). "Full squad is checking Bush case." *Omaha World Herald.* October 10.

Anastasio, P., & Costa, D. M. (2004). "Twice hurt: How newspaper coverage may reduce empathy and engender blame for female victims of crime." *Sex Roles.* November 51(9/10): 535-43.

Armstrong, K., & Lighty, T. (1999). "Death row conviction thrown out: 11th reversal in 12 years will free Chicago man." *Chicago Tribune.* February 20. Page 1.

Baggs, J. (1993). "1993 deadliest ever in Decatur." *Decatur Daily.* August 22. A1.

Baker, M. H., Nienstedt, B. C., Everett, R. S., & McCleary, R. (1983). "The impact of a crime wave: Perceptions, fear, and confidence in the police. *Law and Society Review.* 17: 319-333.

Baldus, D., Woodworth, G., & Pulaski, C. (1990). *Equal justice and the death penalty: A legal and empirical analysis.* Boston, MA: Northeastern University Press.

Baldwin, D. (2001). "Jury hearing testimony in 1980's murder cases." *Daily Oklahoman.* December 6.

Barak, G. (1994). "Media, society, and criminology." Pp 3-5 in *Media, Process, and the Social Construction of Crime.* G. Barak Ed. New York: Garland Publishing.

Barkan, S. E. (2001). *Criminology: A sociological understanding.* Second Edition. Upper Saddle River, NJ: Prentice-Hall.

Barnes, M. (1989). "SBI begins review of Eastburn murders." *Fayetteville Observer Times.* April 27.

Barrett, M. (1989). "Knew it would be a difficult case to win." *Fayetteville Observer Times.* April 20.

Bauerlein, V. (1997). "Rivera receives death sentence." *Winston-Salem Journal.* October 25. B1.

Baughman, C., & Guarisco, T. (2001a). "Justice for none." Part One of Three. *The Advocate.* March 18. A1.

Baughman, C., & Guarisco, T. (2001b). "Justice for none." Part Two of Three. *The Advocate.* March 19. A1.

Baughman, C., & Guarisco, T. (2001c). "Justice for none." Part Three of Three. *The Advocate.* March 20. A1.

Beckett, K., & Sasson, T. (2000). *The politics of injustice: Crime and punishment in America.* Thousand Oaks, CA: Pine Forge Press.

Bedau, H. A. (1997). *The death penalty in America: Current controversies."* New York: Oxford University Press.

Bendavid, N. (1998). "Attendees assail capital punishment: Former death row inmates honored at NU conference." *Chicago Tribune.* November 15. Page 4.

Benford, R. D., & Hunt, S. A. (2003). "Interactional dynamics in public problems marketplaces: Movements and the counterframing and reframing of public problems." Pp 153-186 in *Challenges and Choices: Constructionist Perspectives on Social Problems.* J. A. Holstein and G. Miller (eds). New York: Aldine De Gruyter.

Berdayes, L. C., & Berdayes, V. (1998). "The information highway in contemporary magazine narrative." *Journal of Communication.* 48:109-124.

Berg, B. L. (2001). *Qualitative research methods for the social sciences.* Fourth edition Needham Heights, MA: Allyn & Bacon.

Best, J. (1990). *Threatened children rhetoric and concern about child victims.* Chicago: University of Chicago Press.

Best, J. (1991). ""Road warriors on hair-trigger highways": Cultural resources and the media's construction of the 1987 freeway shootings problem." *Sociological Inquiry.* 61:327-345.

Best, J. (1995). *Images of issues: Typifying contemporary social problems.* Second edition. Hawthorne, NY: Aldine de Gruyter.

Best, J. (1999). *Random violence: How we talk about new crimes and new victims.* Los Angeles, CA: University of California Press.

Bishop, R. (2003). "It's not always about the money: Using narrative analysis to explore newspaper coverage of the act of collecting. *Communication Review.* 6(2) :117-136.

Blanchard, M. P. (2001). "Vigil held to protest Pa. death penalty: A year after a man on death row was acquitted, 250 rallied outside five state prisons yesterday." *Philadelphia Inquirer.* October 21. B4.

Bleed, J. (2001). "Ex-death-row inmate wants Benetton ad cash: Jeremy sheets says the state owes him the $1,000 it confiscated after he appeared in ads." *Omaha World Herald.* October 5. A1.

Bohm, R. M. (2003). *Deathquest II: An introduction to the theory and practice of capital punishment in the United States.* Second edition. Cincinnati, OH: Anderson.

Borchard, E. M. (1932). *Convicting the innocent: Sixty-five actual errors of criminal justice.* New Haven, CT: Yale University Press.

Bosworth, C., Jr. (1990). "Jury deliberates fate of man accused in murder of boy 8." *St. Louis Post-Dispatch.* October 3. A5.

Box, S. (1983). *Power, crime and mystification.* New York: Tavistock.

Braun, B. (1993). "Tulsan cleared in wife's slaying." *Tulsa World.* April 1. A1.

Brown, J. W. (1995). "Family asks freedom for inmate son." *Phoenix Gazette.* August 3. B1.

Bruner, J. (1990). *Acts of meaning.* Cambridge, MA: Harvard University Press.

Brunkow, A. (1997a). "On tape, Barnett says Miss Bush died because of her race." *Omaha World Herald.* May 2. A1.

Brunkow, A. (1997b). "Sheets testifies that he didn't kill Miss Bush." *Omaha World Herald.* May 5. A1.

Brunkow, A. (1999a). "Ruling's meaning for Sheets debated: Nebraskans differ on the effects of a U.S. Supreme Court decision in a similar death-penalty case." *Omaha World Herald.* June 12. A1.

Brunkow, A. (1999b). "Sheets, Virginia cases similar." *Omaha World Herald.* January 28. A1.

Bucsko, M. (1996). "Police feel close to solving Pulaski homicides." *Pittsburgh Post-Gazette.* March, 17. A19.

Bulfin, G. (1990). "On death row, prisoners stall." *Sun Sentinel.* May 11. A14.

Burbach, C., & Powell, J. (1992). "2 disappearances puzzle police." *Omaha World Herald.* September 25.

Bureau of Justice Statistics. (2003). Victim Characteristics . DOJ website publication.

Butler, P. (1991). "Status of other condemned inmates." *The State.* September 6. A8.

Carmines, E., & Zeller, R. (1979). *Reliability and validity assessment.* Thousand Oaks, CA: Sage.

Champaign-Urbana News Gazette. (1997). "Group presses for halt to executions." July 16.

Chermak, S. M. (1994). "Body count news: How crime is presented in the news media." *Justice Quarterly.* 11(4): 561-582.

Chermak, S. M. (1995a). *Victims in the news: Crime and the American news media.* Boulder, CO: Westview Press.

Chermak, S. M. (1995b). "Image control: How police affect the presentation of crime news." *American Journal of Police* 14(2): 21-43.

Chermak, S. M. (1998a). "Predicting crime story salience: The effects of crime, victim, and defendant characteristics." *Journal of Criminal Justice.* 26(1):61-71.

Chermak, S. M. (1998b). "News value of African-American victims: An examination of the media's presentation of homicide." *Journal of Crime and Justice.* 21(2):71 to 88.

Clay, N. (1987). "Suspect says he saw killings of 2 women in dreams." *Daily Oklahoman.* August 15.

Clay, N. (1988). "Jurors decide death penalty in city killings." *Daily Oklahoman.* May 20.

CNN/USA Today/Gallup Poll. (2000). Majority of Americans Believe Innocent Person Has Been Executed in Last Five Years. June 30. Online publication.

Connelly, M. (1985a). "Paroled killer charged in rape of girl." *Sun Sentinel.* April 20.

Connelly, M. (1985b). "Parolee charged in girl's rape." *Sun Sentinel.* April 19.

Cook, T. D., & Campbell, D. T. (1979). *Quasi-experimentation.* Dallas, TX: Houghton Mufflin.

Cooper, C., & Boyd, R. (1995). "3 sought in Quarter killing; Witnesses see killers hop in car." *The Times-Picayune.* March 4. A1.

Cooper, T. (1998). "Taped confession clouds Bush case: Some say verdict may be overturned." *Omaha World Herald.* November 18. A1.

Couch, J. (1985). "Mother, 2 girls found slain." *Fayetteville Observer Times.* May 13. A1.

Coyle, P. (1998). "Port of Call case retrial ordered; Court says teen treated wrongly." *Times-Picayune.* April 15. A1.

Daily Oklahoman. (1987a). "Competency questioned." March 7.

Daily Oklahoman. (1987b). "Man reported competent." May 22.

Daily Oklahoman. (1987c). "Death penalty sought in killings." February 26.

Daily Oklahoman. (1992). "Man awaiting second trial in wife's death." August 13. Page 11.

Daley, D. (2000). Biker given 45 years in 1993 Slaying in Richmond: Ex-Outlaw sentenced for slaying on farm." *Chicago Tribune.* March 10. Page 5.

Death Penalty Information Center (2002). *Innocence: Freed from death row.* Online document.

Death Penalty Information Center. (2003). *Death row facts.* Online document.

Decatur Daily. (1998). "Appeals court upholds two death sentences." December 19. A14.

DeFalco, B. (2002a). "DNA may free 1st Arizonan: Inmate convicted twice in murder." *Arizona Republic.* April 5. A1.

DeFalco, B. (2002b). "Doubts plagued trails [sic] in '91 killing." *Arizona Republic.* April 8. B1.

DeFalco, B., & Wagner, D. (2002). "1st day out as a free man: Inmate saved by DNA dives into life, political debate." *Arizona Republic.* April 10. A1.

Dieter, R. C. (1997). *Innocence and the death penalty: The increasing danger of executing the innocent.* Washington, D.C.: Death Penalty Information Center.

Dodd, S. (1995). "New evidence may free felon." *Phoenix Gazette.* June 2. A1.

Duwe, G. (2000). "Body-count journalism: The presentation of mass murder in the news media." *Homicide Studies Journal.* 4(4):364-399.

East, J. (1990a). "DA unswayed by questions on bite mark." *Tulsa World.* February 28. A3.

East, J. (1990b). "Murder case key evidence is disputed." *Tulsa World.* February 26. A1.

Ericson, R., Baranek, P., & Chan, J. (1989). *Negotiating control: A study of news sources.* Toronto: University of Toronto Press.

Fan, D. P., Keltner, K. A., & Wyatt, R. O. (2002) A Matter of Guilt or Innocence: How News Reports Affect Support for the Death Penalty in the United States. *International Journal of Public Opinion Research* 14:439-452.

Farmerville Gazette. (1986). "Robbery motive in murder." September 11. A1.

Fayetteville Observer Times. (1998). "Notorious crimes. September 14.

Filosa, G. (2002). "DA's office could find itself on defense; Ex-death row inmate still seeking lawsuit." *Times Picayune.* September 6. A1.

Fischer, H. (2002). "Letting juries impose death advances in House, Senate." *Arizona Daily Star.* A4.

Fitzgerald, H. (1997). "Man cleared in 2nd murder trial: Pompano harness worker convicted in '91 of raping, killing fellow groom." *Sun Sentinel.* July 17. B3.

Fitzgerald, T. (2000). "Legislators hear testimony of man freed from death row." *Philadelphia Inquirer.* November 22. B1.

Foushee, B. (1991a). "Judge may let jury inspect death scene." *Tampa Tribune.* October 8. Page 1.

Foushee, B. (1991b). "Man accused of killing wife lied on loan papers, prosecutor says." *Tampa Tribune.* February 28. Page 4.

Foushee, B. (1991c). "Lawyer seeks ex-teacher's release from jail." *Tampa Tribune.* March 20. Page 3.

Foushee, B. (1994). "High court ruling frees prisoner." *Tampa Tribune.* January 6. Page 1.

Frank, J., & Frank, B. K. (1957). *Not Guilty.* Garden City, NY: Doubleday.

Friedberg, A. (2000). "Ex-detective hunted suspect for 20 years: Charges bring vindication for investigator." *Sun Sentinel.* December 16. A8.

Gainesville Sun. (1993). "Lawyers seek death in phone-booth case." June 16.

Gandy, O. H. (1980). "Information in health: Subsidized news." *Media, Culture & Society.* 2(2):103-115.

Gans, H. J. (1979). *Deciding what's news.* New York: Pantheon.

Geimer, J., & Amsterdam, J. (1987). "Why jurors vote life or death: Operative factors in ten Florida death penalty cases." *American Journal of Criminal Law* 15, 1-2:1-54.

Godfrey, E. (1995). "Charges dropped in deaths." *Daily Oklahoman.* February 2.

Godfrey, W. (2001). "Jury hands women's killer death penalty." *Daily Oklahoman.* December 19.

Goldberg, L. (1996). "1 man killed, 1 wounded in shooting at apartment." *Winston-Salem Journal.* March 23. A1.

Governor's Commission on Capital Punishment. (2002). *Report of the Governor's Commission on Capital Punishment.*

Graber, D. (1980). *Crime news and the public.* New York: Praeger.

Greenberg, D. (1992). "Man held in Starke murder." *The Gainesville Sun.* December 10. A1.

Greer, R. (1988). "Dillon trooper slain." *The State.* December 2. A1.

Guarisco, T. (2000). "Two on death row to be freed." *The Advocate.* December 28. A1.

Guarisco, T. (2001a). "Former death row inmate wants to repair cars again." *The Advocate*. January 3. A1.

Guarisco, T. (2001b). "Ex-inmates face hurdles in battle for restitution." *The Advocate*. April 3. B1.

Guarisco, T. (2001c). "Compensation sought for ex-inmate." *The Advocate*. May 23. B1.

Gusfield, J. R. (1981). *The culture of public problems: Drinking-driving and the symbolic order*. Chicago, IL: University of Chicago Press.

Habermas, J. (1975). *Legitimation crisis*. Boston, MA: Beacon Press.

Hall, S. (1984): "The rediscovery of 'ideology': Return of the repressed in media studies." Pp 315-348 in *Culture, society and the media*. Curran, J., M. Gurevitch, and J. Woollacott (eds). New York: Methuen.

Hall S., Critcher, C., Jefferson, T., Clarke, J., & Roberts, B. (1978). *Policing the crisis: mugging, the state and law and order*. London: Macmillan.

Handley, M. (1991). "Myers now swears he lied in McMillian's murder trial." *Monroe Journal*. December 26. A1.

Handley, M. (1992a). "Judge denies retrial motion." *Monroe Journal*. May 28. A1.

Handley, M. (1992b). "CBS examines murder case." *Monroe Journal*. July 9. A12.

Handley, M. (1992c). "'60 Minutes' raises issues in death case." *Monroe Journal*. November 26. A1.

Handley, M. (1992d). "Prison 'hit man' allegedly hired." *Monroe Journal*. February 27. A1.

Handley, M. (1993a). "New trial is ordered for McMillian." *Monroe Journal*. February 25. A1.

Handley, M. (1993b). "Murder probe is active." *Monroe Journal*. November 11. A1.

Haney, C., & Greene, S. (2004). "Capital constructions: Newspaper reporting in death penalty case." *Analyses of Social Issues and Public Policy*. December. (4)1:129-151.

Harmon, T. R. (2001). "Predictors of miscarriages of justice in capital cases." *Justice Quarterly*. Vol 18 (4): 949-969.

Harris Interactive Survey. (2004). "More than two-thirds of Americans continue to support the death penalty." *The Harris Poll #2*. January 7. Online document.

Heath, L. (1984). "Impact of newspaper crime reports on fear of crime: Multi-methodological investigation." *Journal of Personality and Social Psychology*. 47:263-276.

Herald Leader. (2000). "Some question fairness of inmate's trial." February 28. B1.

Hertog, J. K., & McLeod, D. M. (2001) "A multiperspectival approach to framing analysis: A field guide." Pp 139 - 161 in *Framing public life: Perspectives on media and our understanding of the social world*. S. D. Reese, O. H. Gandy, Jr., and A. E. Grant (eds). Mahwah, NJ: Lawrence Erlbaum Associates.

Hill, J. (1999). "Inmate cleared of slaying agrees to be extradited." *Chicago Tribune*. May 20. Page 2.

Hinshaw, D. (1989a). "Camden jury says Manning killed trooper: Capital case enters sentencing phase." *The State*. April 15. C1.

Hinshaw, D. (1989b). "Manning sentenced to death: Farm worker denies he killed S.C. trooper." *The State*. April 16. A1.

Hirth, D., & Jensen, T. (1995). "Death row inmate to have retrial: Court allows DNA tests, affirms value of genetic evidence." *Sun Sentinel*. June 23. B3.

Hochstetler, A. (2001). "Reporting of executions in U.S. newspapers." *Journal of Crime and Justice*. 24(1):1-13.

Holland, J., & Friedberg, A. (2000). "Quiry [sic] of Satz, detectives sought: convictions overturned in murder." *Sun Sentinel*. March 3. A1.

Holmes, S. (1993). "Son faces charges in slayings of couple in McHenry County." *Chicago Tribune*. April 11. Page 4.

Huff, C. R. (2004). "Wrongful convictions: The American experience." *Canadian Journal of Criminology and Criminal Justice*. January. 107-120.

Huntsville Times. (1990). "Husband held in slaying." October 6. A2.

Hutchens, G., & Fischer, A. (2000). "Death row man acquitted." *The Gainesville Sun*. July 18. A1.

Irwin, J. (1985). *The jail: Managing the underclass in American society*. Berkeley, CA: University of California Press.

Jacobs, D., & Carmichael, J. T. (2002). "The political sociology of the death penalty: A pooled time-series analysis." *American Sociological Review*. February 67:109-131.

Jenkins, P. (2000). "Myth and murder: The serial killer panic of 1983-5." Pp 69-91 in *The mythology of crime and criminal justice*. Second edition. V. E. Kappeler, M. Blumberg, and G. W. Potter. Prospect Heights, IL: Waveland.

Johnstone, J., Hawkins, D., & Michener, A. (1994). "Homicide reporting in Chicago dailies." *Journalism Quarterly*. 71:860-872.

Jones, J. (1985). "Arrest 'surprises' Hennis' neighbors." *Fayetteville Observer Times*. May 17. A1.

Kappeler, V. E., & Potter, G. W. (2005). *The mythology of crime and criminal justice*. Fourth Edition. Prospect Heights, IL: Waveland.

Kappeler, V. E., & Blumberg, M., & Potter, G. W.. (2000). *The mythology of crime and criminal justice*. Third Edition. Prospect Heights, IL: Waveland.

Keil, T., & Vito, G. F. (1995). "Race and the death penalty in Kentucky murder trials: 1976-1991." *American Journal of Criminal Justice* 20(1): 17-36.

King, R. W. & Stewart, P. (1986). "Friends bid her farewell." *Monroe Journal*. November 6. A1.

Kivivuori, J., Kemppi, S., & Smolej, M. (2002). *Front-page violence: Reporting on the front pages of the Finnish tabloid press 1980–2000.* National Research Institute of Legal Policy Helsinki Publication no. 196.

Krisher, T. (1985a) "Autopsy: Mother sexually assaulted." *Fayetteville Observer Times*. May 15.

Krisher, T. (1985b). "Affidavit puts Hennis at death site." *Fayetteville Observer Times*. May 17.

Krisher, T., & Jones, J. (1985). "Man charged in triple slaying." *Fayetteville Observer Times*. May 16.

Kuhl, G. (1990). "KC, North, man charged with murder." *Kansas City Star*.

Kuhl, G. (1991a). "Fatal beating, shots described but defense says husband at store when Carol Dexter was slain. *Kansas City Star*. C5.

Kuhl, G. (1991b). "Judge decides on death penalty after jurors disagree on sentence." *Kansas City Star*. C4.

Kwok, A. (1992a). "Defiant killer sentenced to death for 'depraved' bite-mark murder." *Arizona Republic*. November 21. B4.

Kwok, A. (1992b). "Bite-mark expert testifies in slaying trial." *Arizona Republic*. August 5. B5.

Labov, W. (1997). "Some further steps in narrative analysis." *The Journal of Narrative and Life History*. Online document.

LaMendola, B. (2000). "Death row inmate dies of cancer: Appeal halted 1990 execution." *Sun Sentinel*. January 21. B3.

Lane, J., & Meeker, J. W. (2003). "Ethnicity, information sources, and fear of crime." *Deviant Behavior*. 24(1):1-26.

Lash, C. (2002). "From death row to acquittal. Retrial frees suspect convicted in '94 murders." *Pittsburgh Post-Gazette*. May 4.

Leonard, S. (1995a). "Murder retrial focuses on bite." *Arizona Republic*. September 11. A1.

Leonard, S. (1995b). "Hopes of 2 families hinge on trial." *Arizona Republic*. September 22. A4.

Lett, M. F. (1987). "McMillan [sic] is charged with sodomy." *Monroe Journal.* June 18. A2.

Liebman, J., Fagan, J., & West, V. (2000). *A broken system: Error rates in capital cases, 1973-1995.* The Justice Project. http://justice.policy.net/jpreport/

Liska, A., & Baccaglini. W. (1990). "Feeling safe by comparison: Crime in the newspapers." *Social Problems*, 37: 360-374.

Lore, D., Allard, J., & Decker, T. (1990). "Woomer's punishment mourned, applauded." *The State.* April 27. A14.

Lundman, R. J. (2003). "The newsworthiness and selection bias in news about murder: Comparative and relative effects of novelty and race and gender typifications of newspaper coverage of homicide." *Sociological Forum.* 18(3): 357-386.

Manson, P. (1995). "Death-row inmate's conviction overturned." *Arizona Republic.* June 23. B1.

Marsh, H. (1991). "A comparative analysis of crime coverage in newspapers in the United States and other countries from 1960 to 1989: A review of the literature." *Journal of Criminal Justice.* 19:67-80.

Marsh, S. (2001). "'I though I was dying every day'." *The Decatur Daily.* June 1. A1.

Martin, A. (1997). "New trial likely in 1985 murder of young mother: DNA test gives death row inmate hope." *Chicago Tribune.* July 9. A1.

Marx, K. (2000a). "Communist manifesto." Pp. 245-272 in *Karl Marx: Selected writings.* 2nd edition. David McLellan (ed). New York: Oxford.

Marx, K. (2000b). "Economic and philosophical manuscripts." Pp 83-121 in *Karl Marx: Selected Writings.* 2nd ed. David McLellan (ed). New York: Oxford.

Marx, K., & Engels, F. (2000). "The German ideology." Pp 175-208 in *Karl Marx: Selected writings.* 2nd ed. David McLellan (ed). New York: Oxford.

McClain, R. (2001). "Legislators debate killing death penalty." *The Advocate.* March 28:1A .

Mcdevitt, B. (1997). "Witness says defendant bragged about killing woman, 3 children." *Pittsburgh Post-Gazette.* February 4. B6.

Mckinnon, J. (1994). "Girls seen shortly before killings at home." *Pittsburgh Post-Gazette.* June 17. B1.

McMahon, P., & Tzortzis, A. (2000). "Clearing of convict cracks DNA door." *Sun Sentinel.* December 16. A1.

McRoberts, F. (1993a). "Jurors hear, see evidence of couple's violent deaths." *Chicago Tribune.* October 15. Northwest Final Edition: Page 2.

McRoberts, F. (1993b). "Town asks if gentle farmer killed parents." *Chicago Tribune.* April 14. Du Page Final Edition. Page 1.

Miles, M. B., & Huberman, A. M. (1994), *Qualitative data analysis.* Second edition. Thousand Oaks, CA.: Sage.

Miller-Potter, K. S. (2002). "Death by innocence: Wrongful convictions in capital cases." *The Advocate: A Journal of Criminal Justice Education and Research.* September. Volume 24; Issue 6. Pp:21-29.

Mills, S., & Armstrong, K. (1999a). "The inside informant: The failure of the death penalty in Illinois." Third of a five-part series. *Chicago Tribune.* November 16. Page 1.

Mills, S., & Armstrong, K. (1999b). "Yet another death row inmate cleared." *Chicago Tribune.* May 18. Page 1.

Mills, S., & Armstrong, K. (2000). "Judge under fire takes himself off murder appeal: Morrissey once called convict's lawyers 'idiots'." *Chicago Tribune.* January 15. Page 1.

Mitchell, A. (1995). "Butler found not guilty." *The Commercial Dispatch.* December 17. A1.

Monroe Journal. (1992). "Murder story scheduled on '*60 Minutes*' Sunday." November 19. A1.

Monroe Journal. (1993a). "Morrison case was never closed." January 21. A2.

Monroe Journal. (1993b). "McMillian bill fails." May 20. A1.

Monson, M. (1997). "Burrows settlement reported." *Champaign-Urbana News Gazette.* August 12.

Montgomery, M. (1993). "Heflin: McMillian case shows judicial system is working." *The Monroe Journal.* April 29. A10.

Montgomery, M., & Stewart, S. (1993). "McMillian suit seeks $14 million." *The Monroe Journal.* June 10. A1.

Morton, J. (2001). "Sheets is 'breathing easier now." *Omaha World Herald.* May 15. A1.

Mount, C. (1996). "Prosecutors' Gauger appeal denied." *Chicago Tribune.* October 3. Page 1

NBC News/Wall Street Journal Poll. (2000). July 27-28. Online document.

Neuendorf , K. A. (2001). *The content analysis guidebook.* Thousand Oaks, CA: Sage.

Nichols, L. (1992a). "Padgett murder trial set to begin this week." *The Huntsville Times.* April 6. B1.

Nichols, L. (1992b). "Prosecutor tells Padgett trial jury to expect evidence of brutal murder." *The Huntsville Times.* April 9. B2.

Nichols, L. (1992c). "Doctor tells jury victim was stabbed 46 times." *The Huntsville Times.* April 10. B2.

Nichols, L. (1992d). "Padgett expected to testify." *The Huntsville Times.* April 14. B2.

Nichols, L. (1997). "Padgett now free following acquittal." *The Huntsville Times.* October 3. B1.

O'Boye, S., McMahon, P., & Friedberg, A. (2000). "Death row prisoner dies; Now, DNA test clears him." *Sun Sentinel.* December 15. A1.

O'Brien, J. (1992). "Mob informant points to ex-cop: Former gang boss link to killings." *Chicago Tribune.* May 15. A3.

O'Brien, J. (1993). "Ex-cop to be executed for killing associate: Judge calls him 'dangerous man.'" *Chicago Tribune.* November 23. A3.

Parsons, C. (1998). "Ex-cop now on death row wins new trial." *Chicago Tribune.* April 17. Page 1.

Paulsen, D. J. (2003). "Murder in black and white: The newspaper coverage of homicide in Houston." *Homicide Studies.* 7(3):289-317.

Philbin, W. (1995). "Coach offers alibi to teen-ager in quarter murder." *Times Picayune.* April 14. B1.

Philbin, W., & Baker, C. (1995). "Quarter murder suspect rebooked." *Times Picayune.* March 29. A1.

Potter, G. W., & Miller-Potter, K. S. (2002). "Thinking about white-collar crime." Pp. 2-31 in *Controversies in white collar crime.* G. W. Potter, Ed. Cincinnati, OH: Anderson.

Potter, G. W., & Kappeler, V. E. (1998). *Constructing crime: Perspectives on making news and social problems.* Prospect Heights, IL: Waveland.

Powell, J. (1994). "Suspect is focus in student's slaying." *Omaha World Herald.* A1.

Pritchard, D. (1986). "Homicide and bargained justice: The agenda-setting effect of crime news on prosecutions." *Public Opinion Quarterly.* 50:143-159.

Pritchard, D., & Hughes, D. K. (1997). "Patterns of deviance in crime news." *Journal of Communication.* 47:49-67

Protess, D. (1993). *Hate crimes and the press: A refracted mirror.* Chicago: Northwestern University Press.

Quinn, C. (1998). "Man in 2 deaths gets at least 15 years in prison." *Winston-Salem Journal.* November 13. B8.

Quinney, R. (1970). *The social reality of crime.* Boston: Little, Brown.

Quinney, R. (1979). *Criminology.* Second Edition. Boston: Little, Brown.

Quintanilla, R. (1996). "Son convicted of murders sees freedom at cell door." *Chicago Tribune.* March 13. Page 1.

Quintanilla, R., & Mount, C. (1996). "Conviction in Gauger slayings overturned." *Chicago Tribune.* March 12. Page 1.

Quintanilla, R., & Murphy, M. (1997). "17 indicted in trail of violence by biker gang: Gauger slayings linked to robbery by the Outlaws." *Chicago Tribune.* June 11. Page 1.

Racher, D. (1994). "Proud she got killer convicted." *The Philadelphia Inquirer.* July 27. Page 17.

Radelet, M., & Bedau, H. (1987). Miscarriages of justice in potentially capital cases. *Stanford Law Review* 40: 21-179.

Radin, E. D. (1964). *The innocents.* New York: Morrow.

Reilly, M., & Powell, J. (1992). "Authorities say body likely Kenyatta Bush's." *Omaha World Herald.* October 4. A1.

Reiman, J. (1998). *The rich get richer and the poor get prison.* Fifth edition. Boston: Allyn and Bacon.

Rice, M. (1999). "1999: Taking one more look." *Kansas City Star.* December 29. A1.

Rooney, P. (1989a). "Alleged helper offers testimony in murder trial of Villa Grove man." *Champaign-Urbana News Gazette.* June 1.

Rooney, P. (1989b). "Death sentence given for killing of Sheldon farmer." *Champaign-Urbana News Gazette.* August 2.

Rooney, P. (1991). "Death row inmate pegs hope on new testimony." *Champaign-Urbana News Gazette.* September 22.

Rooney, P. (1994a). "Frye role in 1988 murder still puzzling." *Champaign-Urbana News Gazette.* May 17. A1.

Rooney, P. (1994b). "Key Burrows accuser tells judge: "I lied"." *Champaign-Urbana News Gazette.* July 27.

Rooney, P. (1996). "Burrows "free at last" but Frye's holiday put on hold." *Champaign-Urbana News Gazette.* July 4.

Roshier, B. (1973). "The selection of crime news by the press." Pp. 28-39 in *The Manufacture of News.* S. Cohen and J. Young (eds). Thousand Oaks, CA: Sage.

Roth, P. (1990). "Police seek link in suicide, killing of 2 horse grooms." *Sun Sentinel.* August 13. B1.

Ruffin, J. (1986a). "Witness: Hennis cloth, bloody impression may be linked. *Fayetteville Observer Times.* June 24. B1.

Ruffin, J. (1986b). "Agent: Prints at death scene not Hennis'." *Fayetteville Observer Times.* June 17. B1.

Ruffin, J. (1986c). "Hennis is sentenced to death." *Fayetteville Observer Times.* July 9. A1.

Ruggiero, L. (2002). "Doubts plagued trails [sic] in '91 killing." *Arizona Republic.* April 8. B1.

Sacco, V. (1995). "Media constructions of crime." *Annals of the American Academy of Political and Social Science.* 539:141-154.

Schudson, M. (1991). "The Sociology of news production revisited." Pp 141-159 in *Mass media and society.* J. Curran and M. Gurevitch (eds). London: Edward Arnold.

Shaver, K. (1996). "Man's former co-worker charged in couple's killing." *St. Petersburg Times.* January 30. B3.

Shaw, D. (1988). "McMillian sentenced to death." *Monroe Journal.* September 22. A1.

Shaw, D. (1991). "Court examines trial incentives." *Monroe Journal.* January 17. A1.

Shelden, R. G. (2001). *Controlling the dangerous classes: A critical introduction to the history of criminal justice.* Boston: Allyn and Bacon.

Sheley, J., & Ashkins, C. D. (1981). "Crime, crime news, and crime views." *Public Opinion Quarterly,* 45:492-506.

Shell, P. (1987a). "Neighbors on edge over deaths." *Daily Oklahoman.* January 13.

Shell, P. (1987b). "Police seek suspect in women's deaths." *Daily Oklahoman.* January 14.

Sherlock, B. (1990). "On Illinois' death row, 125 murderers face the ultimate punishment." *Chicago Tribune.* September 9. Page 1.

Sigal, L. V. (1973). *Reporters and officials.* Lexington, MA: D.C. Heath and Company.

Silver, J. (2000). "Death row inmate to get new trial: State Supreme Court rules on Lawrence County quadruple murder case." *Pittsburgh Post-Gazette.* October, 21.

Skogan, W., & Maxfield. M. (1981). *Coping with crime: Individual and neighborhood reactions.* Beverly Hills, CA: Sage.

Slater, E. (2003). "Blanket clemency in Illinois." *Los Angeles Times.* January 12.

Smith, M. (1996). "Arrest made in killing of woman, 3 children: Ellwood City man held in 1997 slayings." *Pittsburgh Post-Gazette.* December 24.

Sorenson, S. B., Manz, J. G., & Berk, R. A. (1998). "News media coverage and the epidemiology of homicide." *American Journal of Public Health,* 88, 1510-1514.

Sorensen, J., & Wallace, D. H. (1995a). "Arbitrariness and discrimination in Missouri capital cases: An assessment using the Barnett scale." *Journal of Crime And Justice* 18, 1: 21-58.

Sorensen, J., & Wallace, D. H. (1995b). "Capital punishment in Missouri: Examining the issue of racial disparity." *Behavioral Sciences and the Law* 13, 1: 61-80

Sorensen, J., & Wallace, D. H. (1999) "Prosecutorial discretion in seeking death: An analysis of racial disparity in the pretrial stages of case processing in a Midwestern county." *Justice Quarterly* 16(3):558-578.

Sorkin, M. D. (1989). "E. St. Louis gang member indicted in killing of boy." *St. Louis Post-Dispatch.* October 21.

Springer, K. (1985). "Girl, 8, injured in attack." *Sun Sentinel.* April 16.

Springer, K. (1986a). "Man is convicted in rape, slaying of 8-year-old girl." *Sun Sentinel.* February 1. B3.

Springer, K. (1986b). "Jury recommends man be put to death." *Sun Sentinel.* February 5. B4.

St. Louis Post-Dispatch. (1990). "Execution ordered in killing of boy." October 4. A10.

Starks, C. (1997). "Wisconsin crime led to biker suspects: Police saw similarities between 1995 burglary and Richmond killings." *Chicago Tribune.* June 12. Page 1.

Starks, C. (1999a). "Gang member details slaying of couple." *Chicago Tribune.* March 9. Page 1.

Starks, C. (1999b). "McHenry officials in 1993 case defended: Wrongful-prosecution suit faces a challenge." *Chicago Tribune.* December 14. Page 8.

Stewart, S. (1993a). "State taking a fresh look at murder." *Monroe Journal.* February 18. A1.

Stewart, S. (1993b). "Probe continues; No arrest in Ronda Morrison murder." *Monroe Journal.* April 18. A16.

Stewart, P., & Lett, M. F. (1986). "No arrest made in murder." *Monroe Journal.* November 6. A1.

Stinchcombe, A. L. (1968). *Constructing social theories.* New York: Harcourt, Brace.

Stolberg, M. (2000). "A question of Justice." *Winston-Salem Journal.* June 19. A1.

Strauss, A. L. (1987). *Qualitative analysis for social scientists.* New York: Cambridge University Press.

Surette, R. (1992). *Media, crime and criminal justice: Images and realities.* Belmont, CA: Brooks/Cole Publishing.

Surette, R. (1998). *Media, crime, and criminal justice: Images and realities.* Second edition. Belmont, CA: Wadsworth.

Surratt, J. (1993). "Pace killing suspect said he'd go free, agent testifies." *Decatur Daily.* October 1. A1.

Taylor. J. (1992). "Women told for their safety: Be confident, don't be friendly." *Omaha World Herald.* September 26. A8.

Taylor, L. (2001). "Death-row case now in state's high court: Condemned man's trial was an 'outrage,' defender says." *Herald Leader.* February 16. B1.

Thomson, E. (1997). "Deterrence versus brutalization: The case of Arizona." *Homicide Studies* 1:110-128.

Thornton, A., & Ellis, R. (1986). "City residents' deaths probed." *Daily Oklahoman.* September 5.

Thornton, A. (1987a). "Police add detectives to murder task force." *Daily Oklahoman.* February 11.

Thornton, A. (1987b). "Arrest fails to calm fears in Military Park." *Daily Oklahoman.* February 27.

Thornton, A. (1987c). "Suspect arrested in two murders." *Daily Oklahoman.* February 25.

Tulsa World. (1985). "Man slain; Clues sought in woman's slaying." June 3. B6.

Turnbo, C. (1994). "News at eleven." *Federal Prisons Journal.* 3(3):47-50.

Tysver, R. (1998). "Attorney questions recording: The verdict against Jeremy Sheets in the slaying of Kenyatta Bush is argued before the Nebraska Supreme Court." *Omaha World Herald.* October 6. A9.

Tysver, R. (2000). "New Sheets Trial Ordered." *Omaha World Herald.* September 15. A1.

Unnever, J. D., & Cullen, F. T. (2005). "Executing the innocent and support for capital punishment: implications for public policy." *Criminology and Public Policy.* 4(1) 3-38.

Varney, J. (1995). "Teen indicted in killing outside Quarter eatery." *Times-Picayune.* May 26. A1.

Varney, J. (1996a). "Teen-ager [sic] gets death for killing Slidell man; Family silent in court." *Times-Picayune.* January 31. A1.

Varney, J. (1996b). "Murder trial begins; Trial focuses on time and face." *Times-Picayune.* January 24. B1.

Varney, J. (1996c). "Date sure teen was Quarter killer." *Times-Picayune*. January 25. A1.

Varney, J. (1999). "Police reopen '95 murder case; Dropped leads may get a look." *Times-Picayune*. January 9. A9.

Vice, J. (1986). "Remembering Ronda." *Monroe Journal*. December 4. A2.

Warden, R. (2002). "The snitch system: How incentivised witnesses put 38 innocent Americans on Death Row. Online Document. Northwestern University Center on Wrongful Convictions.

Warden, R. (2003). " Fourteen Illinois death sentences predicated on confessions allegedly extracted by torture." Online Document. Northwestern University Center on Wrongful Convictions.

Warr, M. (1995). "Public perceptions of crime and punishment." Pp 15-31 in *Criminology: A Contemporary Handbook*. Joseph F. Sheley Ed. Belmont, CA: Wadsworth.

Webb, E. J., Campbell, D. T., Schwartz, R. D., Sechrist, L., & Grove, J. B. (1981). *Nonreactive measures in the social sciences*. Boston: Houghton Mifflin.

Weber, M. (1958). "Politics as a Vocation." Pp 77-127 in *Max Weber: Essays in Sociology*. Gerth, H.H., and C. Wright Mills (Eds) and translators. New York: Oxford.

Weber, M. (1968). "The types of legitimate domination." Pp 1-212 in *Economy and Society*. New York: Bedminster Press.

Weber, R. P. (1990). *Basic content analysis*. Second Edition. Thousand Oaks: Sage.

Weiss, A., & Chermak, S. (1998). "The news value of African-American victims: an examination of the media's presentation of homicide." *Journal of Crime and Justice*, 21(2): 71-88.

White, M. (1999). "Judge sentences Osborne to death for brutal killings." *Whitley Republican News Journal*. February 3. A1.

White, M. (2001). "Teenage death row inmate appealing 1998 Whitley County conviction for elderly couple's murder." *Whitley Republican News Journal*. February 2. A3.

White, M. (2002). "Osborne acquitted." *Whitley Republican News Journal*. August 7. A1.

Wilbanks, W. (1984). *Murder in Miami: An analysis of homicide patterns and trends in Dade County (Miami) Florida, 1917-1983)*. Lanham, MD: University Press of America.

Wilkie, L. (1989a). "Hennis acquitted of '85 slayings." *Fayetteville Observer Times*. April 20.

Wilkie, L. (1989b). "Letters: "I did the crime, Hennis doing the time." *Fayetteville Observer Times*. April 27.

Williams, B. Y. (1999a). "Lost evidence a ticket to freedom for husband accused of murder: Clay County continues to look for items." *Kansas City Star*. June 8. A1.

Williams, B. Y. (1999b). "Missing evidence imperils man's third trial." *Kansas City Star*. June 5. A1.

Williams, F. P., III, & McShane, M. D. (1990) "Inclinations of prospective jurors in capital cases." *Sociology and Social Research* 74, 2: 85-94.

Wilson, T. (1993). "Ex-cop, called 'most cold-blooded killer,' convicted." *Chicago Tribune*. October 20. Page 3.

Woolverton, P. (2001). "Pending execution spurs death-penalty debate." *Fayetteville Observer Times*. March 1.

Yanich, D. (1997). "Making the movies real: The death penalty and local TV news." *Crime, Law and Social Change*. 26(4):303-328.

Zeleny, J., & Zuckman, J. (2004). "Kerry, Edwards joust on who can win: Debate features disagreement on death penalty." *Chicago Tribune*. February 27. Page 16.

CASES CITED

Atkins v. Virginia, 536 U.S. 304 (2002)

Barefoot v. Estelle, 463 U.S. 880 (1983)

Furman v. Georgia, 408 U.S. 238 (1972).

Gregg v. Georgia, 96 Sup. Ct. 2902 (1976).

Jurek v. Texas, 428 U.S. 262 (1976).

Proffit v. Florida, 428 U.S. 242 (1976).

Roper v. Simmons, 543 U.S. 03-633 (2005)

Stanford v. Kentucky, 492 U.S. 361 (1989).

Thompson v. Oklahoma, 487 U.S. 815 (1988).

Appendix A

CASE SUMMARIES

1   Robert Hayes   Pompano Park, FL

On February 20, 1990, Pamela Albertson, 32, was found raped and strangled in her dormitory room at Pompano Harness Track. Robert Hayes, 26,[1] was arrested the same day. Both were grooms at the race track. Hayes was convicted in 1991 based on DNA evidence. The Florida Supreme Court reversed his conviction in June 1995, citing faulty DNA testing. Further DNA tests revealed that a hair found in the victim's hand came from a white man. Hayes, an African-American, was acquitted at retrial in July 1997.

[1] The defendants' ages reported here are their ages at the time the crimes were committed.

2   Warren Douglas Manning   Dillon County, SC

On October 30, 1988 State Trooper George Radford, 41, was found in his patrol car, which was partially submerged in a pond. He had been beaten and shot with his service revolver. Warren Manning, 30, was arrested the same day. He was convicted on circumstantial evidence in April 1989. In September 1991, Manning's conviction was reversed by the South Carolina Supreme Court over the trial court judge's inadequate definition of "reasonable doubt." A 1993 retrial ended in a mistrial. He was again convicted in March 1995. The South Carolina Supreme Court reversed that conviction in December 1997 because the judge granted the prosecutor's request for a change of venue, which was to Manning's disadvantage. His fourth trial in 1999 ended in a hung jury. He was acquitted at his fifth trial in October 1999.

3   Frank Lee Smith   Fort Lauderdale, FL

On April 14, 1985 Shandra Whitehead, 8, was critically injured in her home by an intruder. She had been stabbed, beaten, and sexually assaulted. Frank Smith, 37, was arrested four days later based on eyewitness statements. Whitehead died weeks after the attack. Smith was convicted in January 1986 based on eyewitness testimony. Smith's appeals were consistently denied and his execution date was set in 1990, but was delayed by pending appeals. He died of cancer on death row in January 2000. DNA tests exonerated him and pointed to another known suspect in December 2000.

4   Carl Lawson   East St. Louis, IL

On July 28, 1989, the body of Terrance Kelvin Jones, 8, was found in an abandoned church. His throat had been cut. Carl Lawson, 23, the victim's mother's boyfriend, was arrested in October 1989. He was convicted in October 1990. The primary evidence against him was a footprint, a fingerprint, and the fact that the prosecutor argued that the victim's stab wounds were in the shape of the "star" that symbolized Lawson's gang. The Illinois Supreme Court vacated the conviction in December 1994 because Lawson's public defender had been the prosecutor who arraigned him. He was acquitted at retrial in December, 1996 when it was revealed that the footprint and fingerprints were left at the scene when Lawson and others in a search party found the child. Lawson received a pardon from Governor George Ryan in August 2002.

5   Joaquin Jose Martinez   Palm River, FL

On October 31, 1995, Douglas Lawson, 26, and Sherry McCoy-Ward, 26, were found shot and stabbed in their home. Joaquin Martinez, 24, was arrested in January 1996. He was convicted in April 1997, primarily because his ex-wife testified that he had confessed to her. The Florida Supreme Court ordered a new trial in June 2000 because of improper testimony. At retrial, the state did not seek the death penalty because of excluded evidence. The trial court judge excluded the "confession" tape because it was inaudible. He also excluded the transcript of the tape because it had been transcribed by Douglas Lawson's father. Martinez was acquitted in June 2001.

6   William Nieves   **Philadelphia, PA**

Eric McAiley, 20, was shot to death outside his home on December 22, 1992. William Nieves, 26, was arrested in September 1993. He was convicted on circumstantial evidence and eyewitness testimony. He was an admitted drug dealer and the victim worked for him as a drug runner. Further, an admitted prostitute testified that she saw Nieves shoot the victim. His conviction was vacated by the Pennsylvania Supreme Court over ineffective assistance of counsel. He was acquitted in October 2000.

7   Robert Lee Miller, Jr   **Oklahoma City, OK**

On September 3, 1986, Anne Laura Fowler, 83, was found strangled in her home. In the same neighborhood on January 10, 1987, Zelma Cutler, 92, was found strangled in her home. Robert Miller, 27, was arrested in February 1987. He was convicted in May 1988. The primary evidence against him was the fact that he told police he had seen the murders in his dreams. In January 1995, DNA tests excluded Miller as a suspect and indicated another man was the likely perpetrator. At this time, the prosecutor agreed to a new trial and Miller was released from death row. A judge dismissed the charges against Miller in February 1997, but the prosecutor appealed. The charges were reinstated in March 1997. The prosecutor dropped charges against Miller again in January 1998 and filed charges against the other suspect in March 1998. The other suspect was convicted and sentenced to death in December 2001.

8   Shareef Cousin   **New Orleans, LA**

Michael Gerardi, 25, was shot to death during a robbery attempt as he left a French Quarter restaurant on March 2, 1995. Shareef Cousin, 16, was arrested two weeks later. He was convicted in January 1997 based on the testimony of a man who arranged a plea bargain and an eyewitness. Cousin was convicted despite the existence of a time-stamped videotape that showed him playing basketball at the time of the murder. The Louisiana Supreme Court ordered a new trial in April 1988 because prosecutors had withheld exculpatory evidence. The prosecutor had not revealed that the eyewitness had originally told the police that she could not identify the killer because she was not wearing her glasses. The state dropped the charges against Cousin in January 1999.

9   Jeremy Sheets   **Omaha, NE**

On September 23, 1992, Kenyatta Bush, a 17 year-old high school student was reported missing from school. Her body was found 10 days later in a secluded, wooded area. Her throat had been cut. Jeremy Sheets, 18, was arrested in September 1996. He was convicted in May 1997 and a death verdict was returned in September 1997. The conviction was based on the confession statements of Sheets' friend who committed suicide before trial. The Nebraska Supreme Court vacated his conviction in September 2000 because Sheets had been unable to cross-examine the dead witness. The state appealed that ruling and lost. He was released in June 2001.

10   Larry Osborne   **Whitley County, KY**

The bodies of Sam Davenport, 82, and his wife, Lillian, 76, were found in their burning home on December 14, 1997. Autopsies revealed that they had been shot, but actually died of smoke inhalation. Larry Osborne, 17 was arrested on December 31, 1997. He was convicted in November 1998 and given a death sentence in January 1999. The principal evidence against him was the grand jury statement of a witness who drowned before the trial. The witness had provided numerous contradictory statements to police prior to the grand jury testimony. In April 2001 the Kentucky Supreme Court reversed his conviction over the allowed uncross-examined testimony of a dead witness. He was acquitted at retrial in August 2002.

11   Timothy Hennis   **Fayetteville, NC**

On May 12, 1985, police found the bodies of Kathryn Eastburn, 32, and two of her daughters, Kara, 5, and Erin, 3, in their home. All had been stabbed repeatedly and the mother had been sexually assaulted. Hennis, 27, was arrested on May 16, 1995. He was convicted and sentenced to death in July 1986. He was convicted on eyewitness testimony, though the state also used fiber evidence. He was convicted despite the fact that fingerprints found at the scene did not match his or the victims'. The North Carolina Supreme Court granted Hennis a new trial in October

1988 citing the state's "repetitive" use of inflammatory photographs of the victims' bodies. He was acquitted at retrial in April 1989.

12 Thomas Kimbell, Jr.   Pulaski, PA

On June 15, 1994, Jake Dryfuse found the bodies of his wife, Bonnie Lou Dryfuse, 34, their daughters, Jacqueline, 7, and Heather, 4, and their cousin, Stephanie Herko, 5. They were all stabbed repeatedly in Dryfuse's home. Thomas Kimbell, 32, was named as a suspect two weeks later. He was charged with an unrelated theft, but was not charged with the murders until December 24, 1996. He was convicted in May 1998 based on alleged confessions to a jailhouse informant and a hitchhiker. The Pennsylvania Supreme Court ordered a new trial in October 2000 based on the fact that the trial judge had not allowed the defense attorney to cross-examine a witness about contradictory statements. The witness testified at trial that she spoke to the victim on the phone an hour before the bodies were found. She reported that Bonnie told her she had to go because "someone" was pulling into the driveway. In May 2002, the defense was allowed to reveal to a new jury that the witness's original statement to the police was that the victim had to get off the phone because "Jake" was pulling into the driveway. Kimbell was acquitted.

13 Ray Krone   Phoenix, AZ

Kim Ancona, 35, was found dead at a bar where she worked on December 29, 1991. She had been stabbed repeatedly and bitten. She had told a friend that she was meeting "Ray" after work. Ray Krone, 34, was arrested the same day. He was convicted on bite mark testimony in August 1992. He was sentenced to death in November 1992. DNA evidence excluded Krone as a suspect in June 1995. Later that month, the Arizona Supreme Court ordered a new trial because the prosecutor had withheld evidence. Krone was convicted a second time based on bite mark evidence in April 1996. He received a life sentence. In March 2002 additional DNA tests exonerated Krone and pointed to another suspect. In April 2002 he was released from prison and charges were formally dropped.

14   Gregory R. Wilhoit   **Pawhuska, OK**

On May 31, 1985 police found the body of Kathryn A. Wilhoit, 33, in her home. Her throat had been cut and she had been bitten. Her estranged husband was arrested on January 16, 1986. Gregory Wilhoit, 32, received a death sentence in June 1987. He was convicted on bite mark testimony. The Oklahoma Court of Criminal Appeals ordered an evidentiary hearing in August 1990. Based on the findings of 11 other dental experts who said the bite marks exonerated Wilhoit, the court ordered a new trial. In April 1991, Wilhoit was acquitted by the trial judge and released.

15   Andrew Golden   **Winter Haven, FL**

The body of Ardell Louise Golden, 46, was found floating in a lake a few feet from her partially submerged car on September 13, 1989. Despite the original determination of an accidental death, her husband, Andrew Golden, 45, was charged with murder in April 1990. He was extradited from Minnesota to stand trial. The medical examiner testified at trial that the death was an accidental drowning, but Golden was convicted in October, 1991. The state presented circumstantial evidence including Golden's large debt and the numerous life insurance policies he stood to receive upon the death of his wife. In November 1993, the Florida Supreme Court ordered his release because the state did not prove the victim was murdered.

16   Joseph Burrows   **Kankakee, IL**

William Dulan, 88, was shot to death in his home on November 6, 1988. Joseph Burrows, 35, was arrested on November 9, 1988. Two co-defendants testified that Burrows was the triggerman. His first trial ended in a hung jury in March 1989. He was convicted in June 1989 and received a death sentence in August 1989. The male co-defendant received 23 years and the female was sentenced to 30 years. Following recantations by both co-defendants and the emergence of a new alibi witness, the trial judge ordered a new trial in September 1994. Burrows was released on bond at the same time. The prosecutor appealed the decision in an attempt to reinstate the conviction and death sentence. In April 1996 the Illinois Supreme Court ordered a new trial for Burrows based on a lack of evidence. Because the female co-defendant had revealed that she committed the crime alone and had implicated the two men in an effort to avoid the death penalty, the trial court judge ordered the charges dropped in July 1996.

17 Sabrina Butler   Columbus, MS

On April 12, 1989 Walter Butler, 9 months, was taken to the emergency room by his mother. Sabrina Butler, 19, told the hospital staff that her son had stopped breathing and she had attempted to revive him. The child died and Butler was arrested that day. Prosecutors alleged that the child had been beaten to death. Based largely on Butler's contradictory statements made to police and hospital staff, and testimony from the medical examiner, she was convicted in March 1990. The defense called no witnesses and did not introduce any evidence. The Mississippi Supreme Court ordered a new trial in August 1997 because the prosecutor, during closing arguments, had reminded jurors that Butler did not testify. She was acquitted at retrial in December 1995.

18 Gary Gauger   Richmond, IL

On April 9, 1993, Gary Gauger found the bodies of his parents, Morris, 74, and Ruth, 70, in outbuildings on their farm. Morris was found in the motorcycle repair shop. Ruth was in her Oriental rug shop. Both victims' throats had been cut. Gauger, 41, was interrogated for 21 hours by police and then arrested. During the interrogation, he allegedly confessed. Gauger was convicted in October 1993. In January 1994 he received a death sentence. In September 1994 the judge reduced Gauger's sentence to life without parole saying, that he had failed to consider mitigating evidence. An Illinois Appellate Court reversed the conviction in March 1996 citing the lack of probable cause to arrest Gauger. The state appealed the ruling, but the Illinois Supreme Court ordered Gauger released. He was released in October 1996. In June 1997 members of the Outlaws motorcycle gang were indicted for the murders. One of the bikers received 27 to 37 ½ years for the murders. The other was sentenced to life without parole.

19 Randall Padgett   Guntersville, AL

Catherine Cavanaugh Padgett, 35, was found dead in her home on August 17, 1990. She had been stabbed repeatedly and sexually assaulted. Her estranged husband, Randall Padgett, 39, was arrested on October 6, 1990. He was convicted in April 1992 based on a DNA match between his blood and semen found on the victim. The jury recommended that he be sentenced to life without parole, but the trial judge overrode the jury and sentenced him to death in May 1992. The Alabama Court of Criminal Appeals reversed the conviction in January 1995 because prosecutors failed to tell defense attorneys about a conflicting blood test. Padgett was acquitted by a jury in October 1997.

20 Steven Smith   Chicago, IL

On June 30, 1985, Virdeen Willis Jr., 45, an assistant warden at Pontiac Correctional Center was shot after leaving a Chicago bar. Steven Smith, 37, was arrested four days later. He received a death sentence in August 1986. Smith's conviction resulted from eyewitness testimony and circumstantial evidence. In November 1990, the Illinois Supreme Court ordered a new trial citing the state's prejudicial closing arguments. Smith was convicted at a retrial. Citing unreliable eyewitness testimony, the Illinois Supreme Court vacated that conviction in February 1999. The Court barred the state from trying Smith again and noted that the witness had likely implicated Smith falsely because the only other suspect was her sister's boyfriend. Smith was released in February 1999. He received a pardon from Governor George Ryan in August 2002.

21 Ronald Jones   Chicago, IL

Debra Smith, 28, was raped and stabbed to death in an abandoned motel on March 9, 1985. Ronald Jones, 35, was arrested for the crime in October 1985. He became a suspect because he was suspected in another rape in the area. The other victim remembered that the attacker had bumps on his face. Jones was nicknamed "Bumpy" because of the cysts on his face. He was convicted in 1989. The state argued that semen found on the victim matched Jones' blood type. Jones also confessed. In July 1997 DNA tests revealed that Jones was not the depositor of the semen. Prosecutors dropped the charges against him in May 1999. Upon his release, he was extradited to Tennessee to face charges related to his escape from a prison work-release program in 1980.

22 Clarence Dexter, Jr.   Kansas City, MO

On November 18, 1990, Carol Dexter, 50, was murdered in her garage. She had been shot and beaten with a hammer. Clarence Dexter, 48, was arrested the next day. He told police that he found his wife when he returned from the grocery store. His first trial in July 1991 ended in a mistrial. Dexter was convicted at his second trial based on his bloody clothes and circumstantial evidence. The jury could not decide on a sentence, so the judge sentenced Dexter to death in October 1991. In October 1997, the Missouri Supreme Court vacated the conviction because the prosecutor had made statements in court about Dexter's failure to testify. Charges were dropped and Dexter was released in June 1999 because the physical evidence could not be found.

24 Alfred "Heavy" Rivera   Winston-Salem, NC

Michael A. Nicholson, 20, and James E. Smith, 19, were shot to death in the apartment they shared on March 22, 1996. Alfred Rivera, 25, was arrested on May 9, 1996. Three others were also charged. Rivera was convicted and sentenced to death in October 1997 based on the statements of his co-defendants, who labeled him the triggerman. One co-defendant was sentenced to eight years in prison, the others received 15 to 18 years. They each received plea deals for agreeing to testify against Rivera. The North Carolina Supreme Court ordered a new trial for Rivera in April 1999. The Court ruled that the trial judge had wrongfully excluded testimony that Rivera's co-defendants had framed him. He was acquitted at re-trial in November 1999. In December 2001, Rivera was sentenced to life without parole under a "three-strikes" law after being arrested for selling cocaine.

24 Steve Manning   Chicago, IL

James Pellegrino, 31, was reported missing on May 14, 1990. Four weeks later, his body was found floating in the Des Plaines River. He had been shot. Steve Manning, 39, a former Chicago police officer, was charged in February 1992. He was convicted in October 1993 based on the testimony of a jailhouse informant who said Manning had confessed. In April 1998 the Illinois Supreme Court reversed the conviction because the trial court had allowed improper witness statements. Prosecutors dropped the charges against him in January 2000. When he was originally charged, Manning was awaiting sentence in Missouri on kidnapping charges. That conviction was also later overturned due to the use of a jailhouse informant.

25   Gary Wayne Drinkard   Decatur, AL

On August 18, 1993 Dalton Pace, 65, was shot to death in his home. Gary Drinkard, 38, was arrested on September 1, 1993. He was convicted in August 1995 and sentenced to death in September 1995. The main evidence against Drinkard included alleged confessions to three different people. Each received some type of plea arrangement from prosecutors in unrelated cases. In May 2000 the Alabama Supreme Court overturned the conviction and ordered a new trial because the trial judge had allowed the prosecutor to improperly enter evidence of Drinkard's criminal history. He was acquitted at retrial in May 2001.

26   Joseph Nahume Green   Starke, FL

On December 8, 1992, Judy Miscally, 47, was killed by an armed robber while she was working outside as a street sweeper. Joseph Green, 36, was arrested the next day. He was convicted and sentenced to death in October 1993 based on eyewitness testimony and circumstantial evidence. The Florida Supreme Court ordered a new trial for Green in December 1996. The Court cited an over-broad warrant and improper cross-examination by prosecutors. The trial judge later declared the eyewitness incompetent due to diminished mental capacity resulting from drug use and head injuries. In July 2000, the same trial judge acquitted Green.

27   Michael Ray Graham   Union Parish, LA
28   Albert Ronnie Burrell   Union Parish, LA

Callie Frost, 60, and her husband Delton, 65, were shot in their living room on August 31, 1986. Albert Burrell, 31, was arrested on October 12, 1986. He was convicted and sentenced to death in August 1987. Michael Graham, 22, was arrested on October 27, 1986. He was convicted and sentenced to death in May 1987. Graham and Burrell were convicted on the testimony of a jailhouse informant, witnesses who claimed to see them together the night of the murders, and the fact that Burrell's estranged wife testified that she saw him with Delton Frost's wallet. After the convictions, the Attorney General's Office assumed prosecutorial duties and investigated the case. As a result of this investigation, charges were dropped against both defendants in December 2000. The AG's investigation revealed that the jailhouse informant had fabricated the confessions, other witnesses had recanted and revealed that their testimony was designed to protect other suspects, that the prosecutor had suborned perjury and withheld several vital pieces of exculpatory evidence, and that Graham and Burrell did not know one another prior to their arrests. They were released in January 2001.

29   Walter "Johnny D." McMillian   Monroeville, AL

On November 1, 1986, Ronda Morrison, 18, was shot while working at a dry cleaning store. Walter McMillian, 46, was arrested on June 11, 1987 along with a co-defendant. McMillian was convicted in August 1988. The key evidence presented against him included the testimony of his co-defendant (who accepted a plea bargain) and an eyewitness who said he saw McMillian's truck speeding away from the cleaners. McMillian was sentenced to death in September 1988. During a December 1991 post-conviction hearing, the co-defendant recanted his testimony and said he had been pressured by police and prosecutors to testify against McMillian. In May 1992, the judge denied the motion for a new trial. In November 1992, *60 Minutes* aired a story about the case and raised questions about the evidence, the role race played in the charges, and the actions of police and prosecutors. In February 1993, the Alabama Court of Criminal Appeals ordered a new trial. In March 1993 the state dropped the charges and McMillian was released.

Appendix B

LIST OF NEWSPAPERS

Case	Newspaper	City, State
1	Sun Sentinel	Ft. Lauderdale FL
2	The State	Columbia SC
3	Sun Sentinel	Ft. Lauderdale, FL
4	St. Louis Post-Dispatch	St. Louis MO
5	Tampa Tribune	Tampa FL
	St. Petersburg Times	St. Petersburg FL
6	Philadelphia Inquirer	Philadelphia PA
	Philadelphia Daily News	Philadelphia PA
7	Daily Oklahoman	Oklahoma City OK
8	Times Picayune	New Orleans LA
9	Omaha World Herald	Omaha NE
10	Herald Leader	Lexington KY
	Whitley News Journal	Corbin KY
11	Fayetteville Observer	Fayetteville NC
12	Pittsburgh Post Gazette	Pittsburgh PA
13	Arizona Republic	Phoenix AZ
	Phoenix Gazette	Phoenix AZ
14	Tulsa World	Tulsa OK
15	Tampa Tribune	Tampa FL
16	Champaign-Urbana Gazette	Champaign IL
17	Commercial Dispatch	Columbus MS
18	Chicago Tribune	Chicago IL
19	Huntsville Times	Huntsville AL
20	Chicago Tribune	Chicago IL
21	Chicago Tribune	Chicago IL
22	Kansas City Star	Kansas City MO

23	Winston-Salem Journal	Winston-Salem NC
24	Chicago Tribune	Chicago IL
25	Decatur Daily	Decatur AL
26	Gainesville Sun Times	Gainesville FL
27	The Advocate	Baton Rouge LA
	Farmerville Gazette	Farmerville LA
28	The Advocate	Baton Rouge LA
	Farmerville Gazette	Farmerville LA
29	Monroe Journal	Monroeville AL

Appendix C

GENERAL CODE SHEET

1) Case # _____   2) Defendant Name:
3) State: _____   4) Number of Stories:
5) Year to Row: _____   6) Year off row:
7) Year released: _____
8) Date crime: _____
9) Date arrest: _____

DEFENDANT CHARACTERISTICS:

10) Gender: _____ 11) Race: _____   12) Age: _____
13) Prior Felony Offenses: _____
14) Prior Misdemeanors: _____

VICTIM CHARACTERISTICS:

15) # Victims: _____
16) Relationship of multiple victims:_____
Victim 1:
17) Gender: _____ 18) Race: _____   19) Age: _____
Victim 2:
20) Gender: _____ 21) Race: _____   22) Age: _____
Victim 3:
23) Gender: _____ 24) Race: _____   25) Age: _____
Victim 4:
26) Gender: _____ 27) Race: _____   28) Age: _____

CRIME CHARACTERISTICS:

29) Rural/Urban/Suburban: _____
30) Location: _____

31) Context/Motive: _____

32) Relationship between victim(s) and defendant:

_____

33) Other Aggravating felonies 1 : _____

34) Other Aggravating felonies 2: _____

35) Other Aggravating felonies 3: _____

36) Type of Weapon 1: _____

37) Type of Weapon 2: _____

38) Co-defendant: _____ 39) # of Co-defendants: _____

40) Victim Injury 1: _____

41) Victim Injury 2: _____

42) Victim Injury 3: _____

TRIAL CHARACTERISTICS:

43) Change of venue requested: _____

44) Change of venue granted: _____

45) Released on bail/bond: 1st trial _____

46) Public Defender at first trial: _____

47) Special prosecutor: 1st _____

48) Eyewitness testimony: _____

49) Eyewitness identify defendant: _____

50) Eyewitness identify defendant car: _____

51) Did co-defendant testify against defendant: _____

52) Did co-defendant have plea agreement: _____

53) Type of scientific evidence 1: _____

54) Type of scientific evidence 2: _____

55) Circumstantial evidence: _____

56) Jury / Bench trial: 1st _____

57) Jury / Bench Sentence: 1st _____

58) Confession evidence: _____

59) Who Presented confession 1 : _____

60) Who Presented confession 2: _____

61) Defendant testify phase 1: _____

62) Defendant testify phase 2: _____

63) Was race an issue: _____

POST CONVICTION

64) Overturning Court: _____

65) Reason(s) for reversal: _____

_____

66) Incarcerated after ruling:_____

67) How was defendant exonerated: _____

68) How many trials: _____

69) Another suspect charged: _____

70) Convicted: _____

71) Sentence: _____

72) Original defendant file lawsuit: _____

73) Did defendant face other unrelated charges: _____

Appendix D

ARTICLE CODE SHEET

1) story number: _____ 2) case number: _____

3) wave: 1 = crime/investigation   2 = arrest/pre-trial
      3 = trial   4 = post conviction
      5 = exoneration
4) date of story: _____
5) by-line: none _____ staff report _____ AP _____
      staff and AP _____ other _____

Sources:
6) Sheriff _____
7) detective/investigator _____
8) federal officer _____
9) police chief _____
10) other officer _____
11) "police said" _____
12) police spokesperson _____
13) police report _____
14) prosecutor in court _____
15) prosecutor out-of-court _____
16) other prosecutor _____
17) victim family _____
18) victim neighbor _____
19) victim friend _____
20) defense attorney _____
21) defendant family _____
22) defendant friend _____
23) defendant neighbor _____
24) defendant _____

25) other defense attorney _____
26) official report _____
27) judge _____
28) juror _____
29) prior victim _____
30) prior victim family _____
31) expert witness for state _____
32) expert witness for defense _____
33) other defense witness ___
34) other state witness _____
35) alleged accomplice state ____
36) alleged accomplice defense _____
37) court ruling _____
38) politician _____
39) other _____
40) professor _____
41) member of community _____
42) offer no sources _____

43) indicate heinous crime _____

refer to blood: ____	describe weapon: _____
victim injuries: _____	slash: _____
slit: _____	in cold blood: _____
#wounds: _____	defensive wounds: _____
protecting other: _____	heinous: _____
vicious: _____	gruesome photos: _____
slay: _____	violent: _____ other: _____

44) present the police as crime solvers _____
        special equipment: _____
        more cops assigned: _____
        technical investigation: _____
        hours investigating: _____
        multiple agencies: _____
        lab reports: _____
        fed l.e. involved: _____
        special agents: _____
        gathering evidence: _____

police priority: _____
clues: _____
fast arrest: _____
police solved: _____
other: _____

45) present defendant as guilty _____
    eyewitness identified defendant: _____
    co-def claim def guilty: _____
    anyone say def guilty: _____
    physical evidence match: _____
    place def near scene: _____
    say defendant confessed: _____
    polygraph: _____
    line-up identification: _____
    def car identified: _____
    lack of emotion: _____
    victim/defendant relationship: _____
    pattern of behavior: _____
    arrested quickly: _____
    victim afraid of defendant: _____
    put defendant with victim: _____
    verdict: _____
    other: _____

46) Indicate defendant may not be guilty _____
    mention defendant alibi: _____
    mention another suspect:_____
    witness did not identify: _____
    no evidence: _____
    problems with witness: _____
    tell evidence of innocence: _____
    no witnesses: _____
    court ruling: _____
    other: _____

47) present the crime as a public problem _____
       quiet neighborhood: _____
       middle-class neighborhood: _____
       children in neighborhood: _____
       rural/secluded location: _____
       neighbors afraid: _____
       story about fear: _____
       neighbors cautious: _____
       buying guns: _____
       buying security devices: _____
       more police presence: _____
       advice on self protection: _____
       pressure on police to solve: _____
       other: _____

48) present the victim as undeserving _____
       "elderly" victim: _____   child: _____
       good parent: _____   good worker: _____
       'helpless': _____   student: _____
       good spouse: _____
       good community member: _____
       recent tragedies: _____   dreams for future: _____
       christian: _____
       complied w/assailant: _____
       parent of young child: _____
       other: _____

49) victim age: _____

50) make negative references to the victim _____
       drug user: _____   drug dealer: _____
       violent person: _____   criminal: _____
       other: _____

51) present the victim/family as celebrities _____
        scholarship honor: _____
        other honor: _____
        local celebs attend services: _____
        family invited to public events: _____
        story family coping: _____
        family satisfaction with process: _____
        seek family opinion unrelated issue: _____
        other: _____

52) make general negative references to defendant _____
        unemployed: _____   liar: _____
        alcoholic: _____   outsider: _____
        drug user: _____   social class: _____
        mentally ill: _____   school drop-out: _____
        incarcerated: _____   bail refused: _____
        shackles: _____   prison clothes: _____
        intimidating characteristics: _____
        changed story: _____
        negative demeanor in court: _____
        other: _____

53) present the defendant as a thug _____
        non-violent criminal history: _____
        incarcerated for non-violent crime: _____
        parolee for non-violent: _____
        drug dealer: _____
        gang member: _____
        pattern of bad behavior: _____   other: _____

54) present defendant as violent career offender: _____
        animal/beast: _____
        violent criminal history: _____
        parolee violent crime: _____
        incarcerated for violent crime: _____
        evil: _____   killer: _____
        murderer: _____   rapist: _____
        suspect in other crimes: _____
        other: _____

55) present the defendant as an anomalous killer _____
      educated: _____   good parent: _____
      hard worker: _____   honest: _____
      non-violent: _____   no criminal history: _____
      gentle: _____
      positive demeanor in court: _____
      other: _____

56) try to tie defendant to other unsolved crimes _____
      police think crimes connected: _____
      similarities between crimes: _____
      police talking to other jurisdictions: _____
      bodies exhumed: _____
      story theme: _____
      other: _____

57) present defendant as deserving death _____
      violent criminal theme: _____
      detail prior crimes: _____
      prior sentences: _____
      prior victim focus: _____
      say deserves death: _____
      describe prosecutor pleas for death: _____
      judge reason for giving dp: _____
      juror reason for giving dp: _____
      prosecutor reason for seeking dp: _____
      ask how released from prison to kill: _____
      other: _____

58) describe how system works _____
      sentence options: _____
      define death eligibility: _____
      purpose of hearing: _____
      appeals process: _____
      tell pretrial process: _____
      jury selection process: _____
      define other concept: _____

59) present trial as dramatic _____
      crowded courtroom: _____
      where victim family seated: _____
      where defendant family: _____
      extra security in courtroom: _____
      emotion of victim family: _____
      emotion of defendant family: _____
      demeanor of defendant: _____
      demeanor of juror(s): _____
      other: _____

60) present dp as positive outcome _____
      positive reaction from:
      victim family or friend: _____
      prosecutor: _____
      judge: _____
      juror: _____
      community: _____
      cop: _____
      other: _____
      other positive indicator: _____

61) present dp as negative outcome _____
      negative reaction from:
      victim family or friend: _____
      prosecutor: _____
      judge: _____
      juror: _____
      community: _____
      cop: _____
      other: _____
      other negative indicator: _____

62) present appeals as defendant fighting system _____
      negative reaction to appeal from:
      victim family or friend: _____
      prosecutor: _____
      judge: _____

juror: _____
community: _____
cop: _____
other: _____
appeal presented as non-issue: _____
other indicator: _____

63) present appeals process as long: _____

64) present appeals as necessary _____
    negative reaction from:
    victim family or friend: _____
    prosecutor: _____
    judge: _____
    juror: _____
    community: _____
    cop: _____
    other: _____
    other negative indicator: _____
    theme: _____

65) system worked for defendant with reversal _____
    say system worked: _____
    theme: _____   other: _____

66) system failed defendant with conviction _____
    story theme: _____   say system failed: _____
    express regret: _____   admit mistake: _____
    strong evidence of innocence: _____
    anyone blamed: _____   other: _____

67) system failed victim with reversal _____
    story theme: _____   say system failed: _____
    convinced defendant guilty: _____
    court ruling indicate guilt: _____
    other: _____

68) present reversal as legal technicality _____
       say technicality: _____
       describe evidence of guilt: _____
       close vote of court: _____
       quote dissenting opinion: _____
       excluded evidence prevents new trial: _____
       other: _____

69) system failed victim with exoneration: _____
       story theme: _____
       anyone still convinced of guilt: _____
       say system failed: _____
       other: _____

70) system worked for defendant with exoneration: _____
       say system worked: _____ theme: _____
       other: _____

71) present exoneration as technicality: _____
       say technicality: _____
       excluded evidence prevents retrial: _____
       describe evidence of guilt: _____
       other: _____

72) place blame: _____
       prosecutor: _____
       police: _____
       defense attorney: _____
       witness: _____
       defendant: _____
       judge: _____
       other: _____

73) mention limits on retrial efforts: _____
74) present police as incompetent: _____
75) review court as cautious: _____
76) present death penalty as a deterrent: _____
77) present death penalty as honoring victim: _____

78) did story tell defendant race _____
79) tell victim race _____
80) mention a racial issue _____
81) mention the death penalty _____
82) say "death by electrocution" _____
83) say "death by lethal injection" _____
84) mention public defender _____
85) tell reason for reversal _____
86) list charges _____
87) mention secluded/rural location of crime _____
88) mention special prosecutor _____
89) mention anything religious _____
90) effort to change law in favor of defendants _____
91) effort to change law in favor of state _____
92) describe crime _____
93) tell how victim found _____
94) report motive: _____
95) victim job: _____
96) defendant job: _____
97) report date of crime: _____
98) report location of crime: _____

Index